Free Ride

Noraly Schoenmaker is the creator of Itchy Boots, a YouTube channel with more than two million loyal subscribers. A motorcycling obsessive, her journeys have taken her the length of the American continent, from Argentina to Alaska, from the northernmost point of Europe to the southernmost point of Africa, and to some of the least traveled regions of the globe. Trained as a biologist and geologist, she is based in the Netherlands.

FREE RIDE

NORALY SCHOENMAKER

First published in Netherlands in 2024 by Luitingh-Sijthoff as *Keerpunt*

This edition published in the United Kingdom in 2025 by

August Books, an imprint of
Canelo Digital Publishing Limited,
20 Vauxhall Bridge Road,
London SW1V 2SA
United Kingdom

A Penguin Random House Company
The authorised representative in the EEA is Dorling Kindersley Verlag GmbH. Arnulfstr. 124, 80636
Munich, Germany

A CIP catalogue record for this book is available from the British Library.

Ebook ISBN 978 1 83598 275 4
Hardback ISBN 978 1 83598 273 0
Export Trade Paperback ISBN 978 1 83598 284 6

Translated by Bo-Elise Brummelkamp

Printed and bound in India

Look for more great books at
www.augustbooks.co | www.dk.com

Contents

These pages are intentionally left blank.

These pages are intentionally left blank.

These pages are intentionally left blank.

PREFACE

I was six years old when I wrote, in a school assignment, the words: "I want to go hoem." We were supposed to simply write words like "Dog," "cat," and "ball," but—spelling mistake aside—my mind was apparently elsewhere. Back then, I didn't know that I would later spend years of my life trying hard *not* to go home.

I got my first diary not long after these famous words, and I started to write more and more. Not just in my diary, but also stories, which I would print and fold into skinny booklets. I knew I wanted to be a writer when I grew up. When I began exploring the world on my own in my twenties, I recorded my experiences in detailed travel journals. I've reread many of them and watched back a lot of footage from my YouTube channel while writing this book. Some of the conversations I describe in the pages ahead were held in languages I barely spoke, such as Russian. I didn't understand what had actually been said in them until I published my videos on YouTube, when native-speaking viewers would comment on them.

However, I also describe plenty of experiences in this book that I never shared online. Sometimes this was just because I'd forgotten to turn on my camera, but often it was because I was afraid to record myself in scary and vulnerable moments. I was afraid of how people would respond to my ineptitude. So I chose to go through these most difficult parts of my journey alone, without anyone watching. Now, five years after my first motorcycling adventure, I have gathered the courage to share these experiences.

And finally tell the whole story.

PROLOGUE

A WRECK OF BROKEN DREAMS

Spring 2019

It was early April. Spring should have sprung ages ago, but everywhere I looked the ground was covered in snow. I was in northern Iran, in the Alborz Mountains near the Caspian Sea.

"Look, Basanti—snow!" I'd exclaimed at first and rubbed a handful on her tank. But now I was getting worried.

That morning I'd left Sari, the capital of the Mazandaran province. The plan was to ride to the town of Gorgan, which, like Sari, was right on the shores of the Caspian Sea. It had been a gorgeous day, the temperature perfect for someone in motorcycle gear. I was surrounded by vast alpine meadows. This area was known as the Switzerland of Iran—all that was missing was the sound of jingling cowbells. Tall, snow-covered mountains emerged in the distance as the landscape around me changed, the fertile farmland making way for dry sand and stark rock formations. The various shades of green turned to yellows, browns, and blacks. Two shepherds waved at me when I passed them, their sheep around them searching for the last clumps of grass, and I waved back.

It wasn't long before I encountered the first roadblock. It had been an exceptionally wet spring in Iran, and devastating floods and land-slides had already claimed dozens of lives. For three weeks now, heavy downpours had plagued large portions of the country. I had read in the news that these were the worst floods Iran had seen in seventy years.

I was on my way to Badab-e Surt to see the spectacular travertine formations. The white terraces, holding turquoise- and red-tinted water, were located above a natural hot spring, and I had marked it on my map as one of Iran's geological highlights. Thanks to my former job as a geologist, these kinds of rare phenomena have always been irresistible to me.

A large green sign indicated the exit that led to the terraces, which were about four miles away. However, immediately behind the sign a row of boulders blocked the road, and two smaller signs were sticking out of the rubble announcing road work ahead. I came to a stop, and one of the workmen immediately walked toward me. I pointed at the roadblock and looked at him, puzzled. The man said something I didn't understand. He wore a dark green Puma cap, and his beard was trimmed to match the angular shape of his face. He gave me a piercing look and asked me something, but I only caught the word "motorcycle." An older man who was, surprisingly enough, dressed in a suit beckoned me, so I rode forward a few feet toward him. He pointed at a road in the distance and laughed. With some additional gestures he tried to communicate something to me before eventually realizing I didn't understand.

"You don't speak Farsi?" he asked, in Farsi, revealing his bad teeth.

"No," I admitted, shaking my head. I'd only understood the word "Farsi," so I guessed at the rest. Then, to my relief, a young man wearing an Adidas tracksuit and large sunglasses showed up who did speak English.

"I can't go there?" I asked him.

"He says you have to walk from here," he translated.

"Walk," I echoed the ugly word.

"Walk, walk," he repeated. He briefly chewed on a sunflower seed and spat the remains on the ground.

I thanked him and turned around, disappointed. No travertine formations for me today. After a short distance, I stopped to check my phone. Was there really no other way to get there? I zoomed in on the map and sighed. There wasn't. That also meant changing my planned route to Badab-e Surt. I started Basanti and rode at a leisurely pace down the highway toward the snowy peaks in the distance. It was about 125 miles to Gorgan down this road, so I was in no rush.

All went well for a while, until the asphalt abruptly ended and the road turned into an unpaved track. The heavy rains and melted snow had turned it into a slippery, muddy path, pockmarked with large puddles. I rode slowly and cautiously, scared that my back wheel would slide out from under me. The mountains were spectacular, but I was growing too anxious to enjoy the view. There was just water on the road for now, but what if it turned to snow farther down? I couldn't imagine riding through snow without falling immediately, bike and myself included. I realized that at this rate, the last fifty miles would take a very long time.

It was a few hours before I saw another car, and even then it was so far away that it looked like a toy. It crawled toward me along the muddy track, moving even more slowly than I did. Seeing another vehicle reassured me. I felt slightly less alone, and it had to mean that the road ahead was passable. I stopped to signal that I wanted to ask something. The old, gray car, of a make I didn't recognize, came to a squeaking halt.

"Golgan?" I called out. I always felt like I had to raise my voice when I was wearing my helmet.

The driver opened his door. He was a man of around forty, with a short beard and a cigarette dangling from the corner of his mouth. A boy of about ten years old was sleeping next to him, slumped in the passenger seat with his bare feet on the dashboard. A woman was asleep in the back seat. When the door opened, she woke with a start, stretched, and examined me.

"Golgan?" I asked again. He nodded affirmatively, took the cigarette out of his mouth and pointed it in the direction I was headed.

"That way? Okay, thank you," I said. I held up my hand to gesture my thanks as well. I was relieved that he hadn't said the road was closed or blocked, but on the other hand, I wouldn't have minded if he'd given me a reason to abandon this hellish road. The man put the cigarette back into his mouth, shut his door again, and drove on. I watched them slowly disappear from sight in my rear mirror, all the while deliberating as to whether I should just follow them—away from these muddy, snowy mountains where seemingly almost no one dared to go.

"Come on, pull yourself together," I said out loud. "Just keep riding."

I restarted Basanti and pulled away, trying hard not to look at the dark clouds that were starting to gather in the sky ahead of me. I followed the winding road for dozens of miles before finally reaching some kind of plateau covered in fields, which the snow luckily hadn't reached. I turned onto a smaller trail down a mountainside. On my navigation screen, a series of hairpin bends appeared. The road surface was littered with rocks, and the clay-rich soil had turned into mud as slippery as ice. I kept my distance from the mountainside. The rain had caused a few minor landslides and I was worried a boulder or uprooted tree might fall down and crush me.

I crawled agonizingly slowly toward the upcoming hairpin bend. Switching back to first gear, I tried to control my descent with a delicate interplay of my front brake and clutch. I failed and ended up clumsily sliding down the hill in fits and starts. Thankfully, the trail leveled out after the final bend and I reached the valley, still upright and in one piece. But instead of doing a victory dance, I froze. A fierce river churned ahead of me, and all that remained of the bridge I was meant to cross was a concrete ruin. The force of the water had completely destroyed it. I suddenly understood why I hadn't seen anyone on my descent—everyone here probably knew this was a dead end. Everyone but me. With a lump in my throat, I stared at the heads of foam dancing downstream. I swallowed and spent some time peering up and down the river, but I couldn't see any bridges that were still intact. With shaking fingers, I took my phone off the mount and zoomed in on Google Maps. My fears were confirmed: this was the only place for me to cross the river. Or it would have been, if only there had been a bridge. I had to go back, but I didn't know how. Descending down the steep mountainside was one thing, but I seriously doubted if my engine would have enough power to make it back up. My single-cylinder four-stroke engine had less than 25 horsepower, and the bike weighed well over four hundred pounds, not including the extra jerrycans of gas, the luggage, and my own weight.

But above all, I doubted my own skill. Or rather, my lack thereof. What on earth was I doing?

I tried to pull myself together, turned the key, kicked Basanti into first gear, and accelerated. My plan was to pick up speed and ride back up the mountain at a steady pace. It went fairly well at the start, Basanti handling the first two bends so easily that I was starting to hope I'd make it all the way. But the third turn was the tightest and steepest of all, and I lost momentum before I'd even reached it. When the engine cut out, I was forced to dump Basanti on the ground—all I could do was jump off in time to avoid getting crushed under my own stuff. Unbuckling my helmet and pulling it off my head, I sighed, assessing the situation. Basanti had landed awkwardly, half in a ditch, and I knew it would take a lot of effort to get her out. I put down my helmet on a nearby dry patch and paused to come up with a strategy. After some thought, I got down into the ditch and took hold of my left handlebar. Despite pulling as hard as I could, I only managed to move her a few inches before I was forced to give up and let go. I'd been traveling by motorcycle for months now and my back and glutes were strong, but once again this was pushing my body to its limit. Basanti seemed determined to stay where she was.

I tried a different tactic—I took off more than half of my luggage, grabbed my front wheel, and pulled as hard as I could. The handlebars only dug themselves deeper into the mud. I turned them toward me and yanked on the front wheel again. Bit by bit, I pulled Basanti out of the ditch while her side scraped over the muddy rocks. This would leave some serious scratches, but in our current situation, a few nicks didn't matter.

Once I'd gotten her out of the ditch, I made another attempt to stand her up, and this time gravity didn't fight me. "Yes!" I exclaimed, when I succeeded and Basanti was upright again. But my heart immediately sank when I looked up and saw the tight bend ahead. There was no way I'd be able to gain enough speed to make it through there, especially not from a standstill. I decided to walk next to the bike instead of sitting on it, hoping that would at least make it easier to keep her balanced. I started the engine and gently released the clutch with my left hand while accelerating with my right. I gently leaned her against my thigh and pushed on the handlebars, managing like that for a few yards—until my back wheel got wedged between two rocks at the apex of the curve. I lost my balance and had to let go. Basanti crashed to the ground, and this time it was even harder to get her back up. At this point my forehead was covered in sweat. I restarted the engine with gritted teeth.

"Come on," I yelled, unsure whether I was trying to spur on Basanti or myself. "Go!"

But no matter how much throttle I gave, she wouldn't move another inch. I didn't realize what was going on until a foul burning smell reached my nostrils, and by then it was too late—I had expertly ruined my clutch. Kicking out the stand and letting go of the handlebars, I sank to my knees, staring dejectedly at the engine. In record time, I'd turned my bike into a wreck of broken dreams. Only this morning, she had been my faithful companion who had taken me halfway across the world; now she was out of commission, unable to take me anywhere at all.

There I was, all alone, halfway up a mountain, with a motorcycle that was stuck like a stubborn goat, refusing to take another step. I feverishly tried to remember when I'd last passed a village. Or a house. A person. Hadn't I seen a house just before turning onto this hellish road, on the other side of a field? But the memory turned increasingly murky and disjointed with every attempt to bring it into focus. Eventually, I gave up and faced my only option. All I could do was walk up the mountain and find help, any kind of help. It was the best plan I had. All I could think about was how it was my fault that she had broken down.

I tied my luggage back onto Basanti's back, not wanting to just leave my things scattered around in the mud. If someone happened to see it, they might think it was the scene of a violent crime, and I couldn't do that to people—I'd caused enough misery for one day.

Once Basanti looked, again, like my pack mule, I started walking, taking only my helmet with me. I had left the key in the ignition— it wasn't like a potential thief could just ride off on her. But halfway up the road, that suddenly felt like the most idiotic decision ever. My Royal Enfield was my most valuable possession, and I'd coldheartedly abandoned her. By leaving the key in the ignition, I'd basically said: *Here, take her, she's yours.*

"Why am I doing this?" I complained out loud.

Sure, it was my own choice to ride a motorcycle across the Iranian mountains. But I was also here because my life had completely fallen apart, just a few months earlier. And that had not been my own choice.

Careful not to be sucked back to the past, I tried to shift my focus back to my feet, the slippery path and the helmet I was carrying. It was heavy and awkward, and my muscles got tired so fast from carrying it that I had to switch arms every few minutes. I realized that besides the ignition key, I'd also thoughtlessly left my most important bag behind, the one that carried my travel documents, laptop, chargers, and external hard drives. All I had on me now was my passport and my phone. And that helmet.

I hadn't considered my lack of physical fitness when I'd decided to find help on foot—that particular realization only hit me once I was out of breath. I'd gained muscle over the past few months, but I hadn't gotten much fitter. After all, I was spending my days on the saddle of a motorcycle, not running cross-country. Besides, my leather Ducati boots, like me, were totally unsuitable for this climb. Like most motorcycle boots, they were already pretty uncomfortable under normal circumstances, let alone on a steep, muddy slope. The rigid lining chafed through my socks with every step, slowly peeling the skin off my heels. It wasn't long before my back was drenched in sweat and I had to take off my bulky motorcycle jacket. I wrapped it around my waist and stumbled on.

It was now late afternoon and rapidly getting cooler, but my face was bright red. Sweat was now starting to drip from my forehead into my eyes and then onto the ground. With my free hand, I grabbed the hijab that half-covered my hair and hung down over my shoulders and wiped my face with it. There wasn't a soul in sight, but I was petrified of the Iranian morality police and didn't dare take it off. Worried about the incoming twilight, I glanced at my watch and before I knew it, I slipped, almost flinging my helmet down the mountain in my attempt to keep my footing.

I tried not to think about anything as I battled the rest of the way up the mountain. Too worried I'd start playing out various doom scenarios in my head, I focused on my feet instead. If I kept putting one foot in front of the other, I had to come closer to a solution. It took me an hour to cover the same distance that had taken me ten minutes on my bike, but I finally reached the top of the mountain, the plateau stretching out before me. My heart skipped a beat and then performed a double somersault when I realized that my memory hadn't failed me completely. I saw the field, and on the far side: a house. I tried to speed up, but between my boots and helmet, all I could muster was a clumsy trot.

"Hello!" I called out in Farsi when I'd almost reached the house. *"Salaam!"* I only knew a handful of words in Farsi—this was one of them.

I didn't see or hear anyone, so I kept calling as I slowly approached the house. I turned my attention back to my feet, and when I looked up I saw two tiny figures emerge in the distance.

"Hello," I called out again. It turned out to be an older couple walking toward me. The balding man had a gray mustache and wore black pants and a gray shirt. His wife was wearing a long-sleeved red dress that came down to her ankles and a matching hijab that was firmly tied around her face. I quickly fixed my own slipping hijab with my free hand in an attempt to make a respectful first impression.

Once I was a few feet away, they took me in from head to toe, shock written across their faces. For a moment, I didn't know what to say. Then the woman's warm, generous eyes met mine, and they were so full of love and concern that I promptly burst into tears. She gently grabbed my arm and brushed a lock of hair out of my face, smiling at me. It was a genuine smile, straight from the heart. I took her arm in turn and gratefully looked at her through a haze of tears. Her husband said something to me in Farsi, but I didn't know what. I shook my head to indicate that I didn't understand him.

"My motorcycle…" was all I managed to say. Holding out my fists in front of me, I mimed riding a motorcycle. Then I ran my right hand across my throat. "Broken."

They stared blankly at me. I thought I'd just made the universal gesture for "broken," but maybe it meant something different here in Iran. I quickly dug my phone out of my pocket. I scrolled through my camera roll and tapped a picture of Basanti. Pleading, I held up my phone and showed it to them.

"Broken," I repeated, half turning and pointing toward the mountainside. The man nodded understandingly. He patted his chest and said something in Farsi. I thought he was suggesting that he could ride my motorcycle for me. "No," I said desperately, "you can't ride it either, it's broken down!"

But he nodded again and started walking in the direction I'd indicated before. He looked like he was in his seventies, and I felt more guilty and incompetent than ever. I couldn't let this old man wrestle in the mud with my more than four-hundred-pound bike. I handed my helmet to his wife and quickly gave chase. We walked down the trail in silence for a while, side by side, until he suddenly called out to a small figure in the distance. They shouted a few sentences back and a sheepdog came running toward us. Before I knew it, two shepherds and someone who turned out to be the old man's grandson had joined us and we were a party of five. From our attempts at conversation, I gathered that one of the shepherds was the old man's nephew, though I might have been wrong.

The two shepherds looked young and fit, and I started to believe that we would be able to get my bike out of there. I tried to ask if their sheep would stay put, but they just returned confused looks. I held my breath as I came around the final bend and was relieved to see Basanti standing proudly where I'd left her. The two young Iranian men whooped and exchanged a few words. I suspected they were excited by the sight of such a big motorcycle. In Europe, a 400cc bike was nothing to write home about, but to my surprise, people in many other countries were impressed by Basanti. Especially in Iran, where the locals weren't allowed to have a bike like mine, 400cc was usually regarded with excitement. Motorcycles with an engine capacity of more than 250cc were banned from public roads here. Lucky for me, that law didn't apply to tourists. The official reason was to prevent motorcycle drive-bys, but there was a stubborn rumor that the police just didn't want the locals to have faster bikes than they had. So bikes like Basanti were rare in Iran—as was the fact that I, a woman, was riding it. Iranian women are forbidden to ride motorcycles.

Now that Basanti was in sight, the two young shepherds sped up and soon enough one of them had climbed onto the saddle. He seemed to know exactly what he was doing, as he kicked aside the kickstand and immediately started the engine. When he twisted the throttle, but the bike didn't move an inch, I was secretly relieved that I wasn't a complete idiot. I had apparently ruined it so perfectly that he couldn't get it to work either. The other shepherd and I stood on either side, placed our hands on the luggage cases and pushed hard. Slowly but surely she started to move, and then he rode off as if it had been him, not me, who had traveled more than 9,000 miles on this motorcycle. The old man beamed at me. I laughed and gently squeezed his arm.

"*Merci*," I said and looked at him. *Thank you.* The four of us began the pursuit after Basanti and her new rider, but it wasn't long until we caught up with him—he'd stalled just after the next bend. This time we didn't manage to get Basanti going, so we had no choice but to push her all the way up the path. The three younger men and I took turns to give our tired bodies a chance to recover, while the old man acted as our sweeper and followed behind us.

By the time we reached the plateau, I could barely see the field and the house. It had gotten so late that twilight and then total darkness had caught up with us. The kind old lady came out to meet us when we'd almost reached the house, and then briskly brought all five of us inside. None of us protested.

She showed me my room for the night. It was almost completely empty, except for a small cabinet. The floor was covered by a high-pile red rug surrounded by plump, colorful cushions. I smiled at her and she showed me the bathroom where I could freshen up. I was so exhausted that I wanted to sink onto the floor and fall asleep then and there. But I was dirty, and I reeked so badly that it would have felt criminal to touch the beautiful rug in my current state.

I dragged myself into the bathroom, where I glanced into the small mirror to assess the damage. I felt my jaw drop. I looked like a scarecrow. My cheeks were covered in smudges, my mascara had run, one of my drawn-on eyebrows had disappeared, my hijab was gross and only covered half my hair, which was stuck to my forehead in dusty clumps. No wonder the sight of me had scared them when they first saw me.

PART 1

The unpaved road had become my new obsession.

Chapter 1

THE WEDDING

November 2018

It was the night before my departure, and I carefully laid out my motorcycle gear on the edge of my bed, just like my mother used to do with my clothes when I was a kid. I'd been staying in a small room in Hotel Cosmo for a month, just outside the Karol Bagh area in Delhi, and after all that time I thought of this bed with its tacky black headboard as my own. I examined the outfit at length. My slightly worn Ducati boots, a dark gray pair of Kevlar motorcycle pants, the knee protectors every motorcyclist in India seemed to wear and that tied on over my pants, my black motorcycle jacket, a pair of black leather gloves, and my Ducati helmet.

I had flown back to the Netherlands for no other reason than to pick up my international motorcycle license, and had decided to pick up my riding gear while I was at it. It felt ridiculous to fly halfway across the world just to pick up a few things, and it had taken a large chunk out of my budget—money I couldn't really afford to lose.

Buying that plane ticket had been the last thing I'd wanted to do. I'd left the Netherlands three months earlier thinking that I'd be gone for at least a few years. Going back so quickly had felt like a failure, and besides my parents and two close friends, I hadn't told anyone I was in the country. I briefly stopped by my storage unit to dig out my riding gear and bought an international license at the travelers' association store. The latter felt like a complete joke; what self-respecting license is simply for sale in a shop? But without this piece of paper—which was basically just a translation of my Dutch license—I wasn't insured and that was a risk I wasn't willing to take. My parents had been unyielding on that front from the moment my older brother bought his first moped at sixteen.

"If you seriously injure someone while riding without insurance, it will bankrupt us and we'll have to sell the house," had been my mother's endless, stern refrain. This speech, to my teenage ears a rather melodramatic one, always annoyed me to no end, but apparently it had sunk in. So much so that I was now spending more than one thousand euros on a return ticket to the Netherlands just to buy an international motorcycle license.

Back in India, I looked at a map of the country, which I'd finally managed to find in a small bookshop on Arya Samaj Road in Delhi, that was now spread out next to my gear. Why did I never manage to fold these things back properly after using them? I fiddled with it for a while, tapped the map a few times to get the folds in the right place, then sighed.

I was about to leave Delhi with the absurd plan of riding my motorcycle to Malaysia. After thoroughly inspecting my map, that seemed to be the most logical destination. India and Pakistan hated each other with a passion, so it looked like a bad idea to ride west to Pakistan on a motorcycle with an Indian license plate. China doesn't allow foreigners free travel with a non-Chinese vehicle, so the north wasn't an option. With only more of India to the south, all that was left was to ride east, which had the benefit of feeling like a relatively safe option. Years before, I'd traveled extensively through Myanmar, Thailand, Laos, Cambodia, Vietnam, and Malaysia on a solo backpacking trip, so I was at least familiar with that part of the world.

I couldn't sleep from all the excitement, and after a restless night of tossing and turning, my alarm went off at 6 a.m. I took a quick shower, got dressed, and slung my backpack over my shoulder. It was heavier than I'd hoped, even after I'd taken out two books the night before: a trashy novel another traveler had given me and *Papillon*, one of my favorite books. Not wanting to part with any of my other belongings, I sped through the whitewashed hotel hallway and took the elevator downstairs. I descended the five steps outside the hotel to my bike and put my backpack down. The air was warm and sweet. It smelled like India: like incense, fresh *pani puri* sold by countless street vendors, and cow shit. I was convinced that if you blindfolded me and took me to ten different countries, I'd instantly know which one was India. I briefly caressed my motorcycle's white gas tank, like petting a fat white cat.

"Are you ready, Basanti?" I whispered quietly. I'd had a custom name decal made at the very last minute and stuck it on the front mudguard. I'd decided to christen my brand-new bike "Basanti" after the heroine from *Sholay*, a famous Indian movie. Everyone in India knew it, and Basanti's heroine status was exactly what I needed. If there would be moments in my journey when I couldn't be the heroine, at least I would have Basanti.

The two managers of Hotel Cosmo came outside to see me off. Long-term tenants were nothing unusual in their hotel. I'd noticed a few days into my stay that almost all other guests had serious head wounds or bandaged limbs; some were even in wheelchairs. I found out they had all come from war zones in Iraq or Afghanistan, and the owners would arrange transportation to and from the hospital in Delhi for them. Although my reasons for staying there were of a different nature, they had welcomed me with open arms and were sorry to see me go.

If it had been up to me, I never would have stayed there for a full month. The terrible air quality in India's capital had earned Delhi the undesirable title of "most polluted city in the world." I hadn't seen a single blue sky the entire month. Every day, millions of people woke up under a gray blanket of heavy smog in this place. I hated it, but I didn't have much choice. I had bought a brand-new Royal Enfield Himalayan motorcycle, and thanks to India's notorious bureaucracy it took thirty days before I'd received the permanent license plate and registration documents.

Hotel Cosmo was a stone's throw from Karol Bagh, which was the perfect neighborhood for me to stay in during my month in Delhi. In India, there are usually bazaars for everything: markets where you can only get perfume or spices or flowers. Shop owners deliberately choose to open their businesses next door to their direct competition. So if I wanted a secondhand book, I had to go to Arya Samaj Road. Or if I needed new clothes, I made my way to Ajmal Khan Road. But Karl Bagh was known as the motorcycle neighborhood. New motorcycles, secondhand motorcycles, accessories, clothing, tours, and repairs—they had it all. I soon found out that Naiwala Street was completely dedicated to Royal Enfield. In the eighty small shops lined up on either side of the street, a Royal Enfield owner could find anything their heart desired.

I'd grown used to the chaos and noise of a city like Delhi by this point, but Naiwala Street seemed to step it up a notch. The street itself was barely visible among the abundance of motorcycles, pedestrians, wooden carts pulled by either people or animals, *tuk-tuks*, food stalls and motorcycle parts on display. But it wasn't long before I became a fixture of Naiwala Street myself. I decided to spend my time gaining some essential repair skills. To me, motorcycle maintenance was like a secret language that only the bikes themselves spoke, drawing from a dictionary written in hieroglyphics. I met Satnam, a man who worked at Shakti Accessories and who was willing to teach me the basics. He had a short goatee and a couple of deep scars on his left cheek. His calm disposition made me trust him. In exchange for his lessons, I bought all the accessories we installed on my motorcycle in his shop.

"I just don't have the additional headlights," Satnam said, clearly disappointed. Then his face brightened. "My cousin has a shop, he does sell them. Come, come, I'll take you," he said over his shoulder while making his way to his moped. "Come," he said encouragingly. I hesitated. I wasn't overjoyed at the prospect of riding pillion with him. I wanted those lights though, so I reluctantly agreed. I'd only just grabbed hold of the grips on the back when he revved the engine and the shabby moped lurched into motion. He skillfully navigated the small streets and kept narrowly avoiding pedestrians, motorcycles, and once even a cart full of gas canisters.

"Hold on," he yelled over his shoulder.

"What do you think I'm doing!" I yelled back.

The traffic churned through the streets, everyone miraculously finding their way without ever coming into contact with each other. It was a perfectly orchestrated ballet and an occasionally raging dance. He indicated where he was going by way of furiously beeping his horn. The sound of a thousand claxons was the common language here, one I barely spoke. Even without understanding it, I could feel the hustle and bustle of Delhi's streets. It was a vibrant mixture of colors and smells. Of people, from poor to middle class, from women with woven baskets on their heads to chai-sellers and holy men. Everything was intense in India, nothing moderate or meandering. People lived passionately here, with an ardor that both intrigued and frightened me. Everywhere I looked the street was stained red, not by the bloody remnants of violent crimes but by spat-out *paan*, a kind of chewing tobacco. People loudly cleared their throats, belched, gargled, and openly relieved themselves. But from the back of the moped I also saw laughing faces flash by and heard popular Bollywood music being blasted out of speakers. Teenagers walked down the street with their arms around each other, or were stuffed into rickshaws by the dozen, chattering excitedly.

We came to a stop with another lurch, like the one at the start of our journey. I climbed off the moped, happy to have arrived in one piece. Satnam ushered me into his cousin's shop and began to speak with him in rapid Hindi. His cousin listened closely, all the time taking me in from the corner of his eye. Then he ducked into the stockroom, quickly reappearing with a box of lights.

"How much are these?" I asked him directly.

"Three hundred rupees," he said, avoiding my gaze.

"Two hundred fifty," I countered, bobbing my head. I'd mastered the head-bob on my first trip through India. I knew when to do it, if it should be subtle or forceful, and when to stop. It could mean anything: *yes, no, maybe, alright then, hello,* and *goodbye*—just to name a few options.

"Two hundred fifty," the cousin said, bobbing back at me. The deal had been made. We were about to race back to our corner of Karol Bagh when the cousin's wife appeared.

"Chai?" she asked. I wasn't about to turn that down, so we stayed to drink a cup. The woman and I had a conversation I'd had hundreds of times before. It went like this:

"Which country?"

"The Netherlands."

"Your good name?"

"Noraly."

"Are you married?"

"No."

She looked at me more intensely and her gaze was of desperate sadness. "How old are you?"

"Thirty-one."

And then, silence. She didn't have to say anything. Her thoughts were so loud I could hear them: *Thirty-one and unmarried? What's wrong with her?* Satnam had overheard our conversation and quickly came to my aid.

"People in Europe don't marry until they're *very* old. Sometimes they don't marry at all!" I gave him a grateful look. The woman nodded pensively and asked her husband something in Hindi. It seemed she'd asked about my bike.

"You alone, you free," she said eventually.

"That's right," I said, delighted she understood. "I'm free." I smiled at her.

"But no husband, no children, very sad," she added, and sorrowfully cast down her eyes. I looked at Satnam, then at my empty cup. I cleared my throat and stood up. It was time to go.

Back on our street in Karol Bagh, my Basanti got a new, louder exhaust, crash guards to protect her engine, two gallon-sized jerrycans, a leather seat cover, hand guards, handlebar risers, and the two additional headlights we'd just bought. Satnam taught me how to change the clutch cable, fuses, brake pads, oil, and oil filter. How to grease and tension the chain, clean the air filter, change the tires, and remove the battery. I stood next to him, nodding earnestly and taking pictures of everything he did.

Two weeks later, I'd finished my crash course in motorcycle mechanics, confident that in a pinch, I wouldn't be able to repair anything whatsoever. I lacked all talent.

It was during that time that I found out there was something else I needed besides my license plate and registration documents: a Carnet de Passage. I had done some online research and learned that apparently I'd need this yellow booklet to enter Myanmar. As far as I understood, it was kind of like a passport for my motorcycle that proved to customs officials of other countries that I wasn't secretly importing my bike, but that I would leave the country with it in the short term. I found a phone number for the Mumbai branch of the WIAA, the Western India Automobile Association, and called it.

"WIAA, Simran speaking. How may I help you?" a friendly woman's voice sounded on the other end of the line.

"Good morning, this is Noraly Schoenmaker. I'd like to request a Carnet de Passage for my motorcycle."

"Good morning, miss, we can definitely help you with that. Are you in Mumbai?"

"No, I'm in Delhi," I replied.

"Delhi, what a coincidence! Our president happens to be in Delhi at the moment, I'll see if I can get you an appointment for tomorrow. It will have to be then, as he will return to Mumbai the day after."

I frowned. Did I really need a personal appointment with the president of the WIAA? That seemed a little weird, but Simran sounded pretty convincing. I gave her my email address, and she promptly sent me the appointment details and a list of what to bring. Just like that, I had a 12:15 appointment for the following day with one Mr. Dossa at the Vega restaurant on Connaught Circus. I carefully read the long list she'd sent. A detailed description of the route I would take, a copy of my passport and motorcycle license, contact details of two family members, a copy of my registration documents, photographs of my bike (left, right, front, and back), insurance details, a list of spare parts and their value, membership of the WIAA, and if my motorcycle wasn't registered to me, a letter containing the photocopied ID of the person it was registered to. I established I could get all the items on the list myself, except for the last one. I'd have to give Irfan another call.

No matter how much I wanted it to be, my motorcycle wasn't registered to my name. Instead, it was registered to someone I'd met just two weeks ago: Irfan Achmad. As a tourist in India, I couldn't just register a vehicle to my name, so Irfan had done it for me. In fact, without Irfan I never would have considered buying a motorcycle in India in the first place.

We met in Srinagar, a city in Kashmir, in northern India. The two of us had both been guests at a Kashmiri wedding. Irfan was a distant relative of the bride, Inshah, and I had been invited by her uncle. The presence of foreigners at a wedding was seen as a status symbol here, but I was so fascinated by the festivities that I didn't particularly care why I had been invited.

I'd bought a beautiful purple Kashmiri-style *salwar kameez* to wear. The *kameez* was a long tunic that reached down to my calves, and the *salwar*, wide-legged pants, were worn underneath. The set came with a matching *dupatta*, a long piece of thin fabric that is draped over the chest and head. There were hundreds of guests at the wedding, divided between two marquees that were each large enough to host a small circus. The floor had been meticulously decorated with gorgeous Persian rugs in a wide variety of colors, and the walls were covered in flowers and fluffy fabrics. You could tell they were marquees from the outside, but inside I found myself in a Persian palace.

I wondered how we would pass the time for three days, but it became clear soon enough. A separate tent had been put up next to the marquees, where gigantic pots were bubbling over open fires. A team of cooks was bustling around, rushing to prepare the *wazwan*—the wedding meal. This was my very first *wazwan*, and to my astonishment, it turned out to be a culinary marathon consisting of sixty-three courses. Now I knew what we'd be doing all this time: eat, digest, and then eat some more.

"Are you veg or non-veg?" one of the servers asked me as I sat cross-legged on a rug.

"Non-veg," I replied. I was sitting next to Deepshikha, who knew Inshah from university. She had come to the wedding with the rest of their friend group, who were all recent economics graduates. Apart from Deepshikha, they were all guys: Shlok, Aquib, Asjad, Harisankar, and Sahabuddin. It took me a while to remember their names. In the weeks following the wedding, I met up with the group a few times to grab a bite in Delhi. I quite enjoyed having friends while I was staying in one place. I quickly realized that Shlok was their ringleader, and he was the one who adopted me into the group.

Men and women ate the *wazwan* separately, so I sat with Deepshikha and two other women whose names I didn't know as each new course was served. Every dish was shared by four people, and the next course was served before the plate was even empty. With sixty-three courses to go, the main focus was eating as quickly as possible. I licked the fingers of my right hand as subtly as I could—I hadn't quite mastered the art of eating with one hand, and I was making a total mess. Some dishes were easy, like *gushtaba*, which were small lamb meatballs in a yogurt sauce. But it was considerably harder to eat my *modur pulao* aromatic pilaf with dried fruit and saffron, with any semblance of elegance. I ate half a plate of *rogan josh*, a spicy meat curry with cardamom, cinnamon, and Kashmiri chillis. I had *dum aloo*, spiced potatoes, and *waza kokur*, roasted chicken marinated in yogurt. I didn't know the names of most dishes, let alone what was in them, but I made sure to try all sixty-three courses. I'd never eaten this much lamb in my life, and by the time the last few courses were served I only reluctantly managed to stuff little bits into my mouth.

In the evening, the guests were driven to various houseboats on Dal Lake, just outside Srinagar. I stayed with Inshah's university friends on a houseboat that belonged to her uncle Hamid, who everyone referred to as simply "Uncle." The boat, which was made of local cedar wood, had been decorated with antique wooden furniture and thick rugs covering the floor. The outside of the boat was decorated with intricately carved patterns of incredible craftsmanship. A set of stairs led to the upper deck, which had a stunning view of the lake and the surrounding mountains. At the back of the boat there was a small dock where you could board a *shikara*, a wooden gondola, to take a relaxing tour of the lake. I had been given my own room, and my tummy was so full that when I lay down on the bed for a moment, I instantly fell asleep.

On the second day, I'd just started a short walk around the tent in an attempt to digest the huge quantities of food when somebody walked up to me. He was in his mid-thirties, had a short beard and introduced himself as Irfan. He asked me how I had come to be invited to the wedding, and I told him that I'd met "Uncle" a few weeks before while traveling through Kashmir on my motorcycle. "Your motorcycle," he repeated, raising a surprised eyebrow.

"Yes, I rented a Royal Enfield in Manali and toured on it for three weeks. Through Ladakh, Zanskar, Kashmir, Jammu, and then back to Manali. It was amazing. I really miss it now that I don't have my own transport anymore," I added.

"Why don't you just buy one?"

"I can't," I quickly replied. "Tourists can't register motorcycles here. I already looked into it."

"Why don't I help you? I can buy it and register it to my name. You give me the money, and then it's yours. I've done it for people before," he said with a shrug. He made it sound so easy that I instantly got excited.

"Okay." I nodded. "Yes, let's do it." We shook hands on it and the deal was done. Irfan lived in Delhi, so all I had to do was book a plane ticket from Srinagar to Delhi and buy the motorcycle off him there. Besides being thrilled about the prospect of having a motorcycle again, I was also glad to know where I was going after the wedding—until then, I hadn't had a clue. It was my new friend Shlok who suggested I name the bike "Basanti."

"Everyone in India knows Basanti, and that movie. It's a good name," he assured me.

–

While I was making a verbal agreement to buy a motorcycle on one side of the marquee, the bride was opening gifts from close family on the other. I watched from a distance as glittering gold necklaces and bracelets were produced. She received leather handbags, silk clothes, and luxury perfumes. That was the moment I finally realized that I was attending a wedding hosted by one of the richest families in Kashmir. I prayed they wouldn't unwrap my gift anytime soon, because I'd bought the bride a tea set. Everyone I'd asked for advice had assured me that this was an excellent gift, but a feeling started to creep up on me that it wouldn't be quite up to this family's standards. Before it was my turn, I quickly taped an envelope with money and a handwritten note to the wrapping paper. In the note, I expressed my deep gratitude for the invitation and how honored I was to be there. I'd also added that the food had been delicious, just to be on the safe side. The note turned out to be a stroke of genius, and to my great relief it overshadowed the modest tea set.

On the third evening, the husband finally arrived, accompanied by eighty guests of his own. Up until that point, the bride and groom had celebrated separately. Now that the actual ceremony was finally starting, I saw the groom for the first time. He was wearing a red turban decorated with gemstones and a long-sleeved white *pheran*, a kind of tunic. His waistband was made of pashmina, the finest and most expensive type of cashmere, embroidered with gold thread. If someone had told me he was a prince, I would have believed them. The ceremony began. The groom and his father sat on the stage in the beautiful marquee. The bride was there too, but she was behind a curtain, hidden from the guests. First, the imam read out the marriage contract in Arabic. Then he asked the groom if he wanted to marry the bride three times. He answered "yes" three times. He asked the bride the same question, and we heard her confirm three times from behind the curtain. Then they were married, and just like that the wedding was over. The groom and his family, now accompanied by the bride, returned to their home, leaving their guests behind. The bride had now joined a different family.

–

Irfan picked up the third time I called.

"I need a picture of your ID," I said. I didn't beat around the bush.

"Excuse me?" Irfan asked.

I told him about the Carnet de Passage and the appointment I had the following day. He didn't seem too keen on sending me a picture of his ID, but thankfully some convincing got him to agree.

The next day, I rode to Connaught Circus. Mr. Dossa hadn't arrived yet, so I went ahead and sat down. I put my helmet on the table and nervously fidgeted with the clasp. How did I suddenly have a lunch date with the president of the Western India Automobile Association, just because I needed a piece of paper to get through customs? Luckily, it wasn't long before a middle-aged man with a neat, manicured gray beard and full gray eyebrows introduced himself and sat down across from me.

"My name is Nitin Dossa, I'm the president of the WIAA," he said, and gave me a firm handshake. After years of working in the mining and dredging industry, I had learned that the first handshake established dominance. A weak handshake: submissive. Crushing the other person's hand, preferably while pulling them toward you: dominant. I subtly tried to crush his hand.

"Pleasure to meet you. Noraly."

Mr. Dossa rummaged around in the briefcase he'd brought with him and looked me up and down. He seemed a little surprised that it was a woman opposite him asking for motorcycle documents.

"How old are you?"

"Uh, thirty-one," I replied. He nodded sternly. After a brief third-degree about my job (I lied) and where exactly I was from (I was honest), we moved on to the business part of the meeting. I slid the envelope containing the requested documents to his side of the table and gave him a stack of bills: one hundred thousand rupees. Simran had already informed me over the phone that I'd have to pay the nonrefundable sum of one lakh, or one hundred thousand rupees in cash, and another two lakh (two hundred thousand rupees) on top of that cash as a security deposit, which I'd get back if I returned my motorcycle to India within a year.

Without blinking or counting the money, the gigantic stack of bills disappeared immediately into his jacket pocket. Apparently, he trusted me. We ordered a *thali*, a large platter of rice accompanied by a range of side dishes, and made small talk about his family and career.

"You have to pay another two hundred thousand rupees," he reminded me again. "I'll be back in Delhi next week, make sure you have the money then and you'll get the Carnet."

He kept his word. Exactly a week later, we met again at the Vega restaurant. This time we just drank a *lassi*, I handed him another two hundred thousand rupees in cash and he gave me the coveted yellow booklet. It wouldn't have surprised me if he had tried to flirt with me, seeing how this was our second date. But Mr. Dossa remained professional, and I could only conclude that this was apparently how things were done here.

–

Now, the Cosmo hotel managers watched me from the steps as I wrestled with my backpack, waiting for me to set off. I lifted it off the ground, slipped it into its black coverbag, zipped it up, and swung it onto Basanti's passenger seat. My blue motorcycle cover didn't fit into my bag, so I half folded it and draped it across the top. Then I took the bungee cords I'd bought at the market and began securing them over my bag. *Why haven't I practiced this?* I thought to myself as I tried to work out where to attach the cords now that the luggage cases were attached to my bike. Despite the fact that I'd already had my baptism by fire of more than 1,800 miles on a rented motorcycle, I still felt just as inexperienced and clumsy as I had back then.

Chapter 2

Baptism by Fire

September 2018

"I'm going traveling," I mumbled nervously. I was sitting on my parents' couch, fidgeting with the hem of my T-shirt.

"Oh, we knew you would," my father replied. He sat leisurely in his armchair and smiled at me.

"What do you mean, you knew?" I asked.

My mother chuckled. "Well, we know our daughter."

I hadn't expected the fairy tale to end. I hadn't expected to be selling my house with no cause for celebration, and instead to be driving home from the notary's office numb and alone. I would sell my motorcycle, a Ducati Monster 796, back to the dealership the following week. I was about to quit my job. Now that I'd lost my house—and with it my mortgage commitment—I couldn't think of any reason to keep working for my boss. I'd promised my cousin Laura she could have my small car, a secondhand brownish-orange Kia Picanto.

There wasn't much left of my current life, all things considered.

But what felt like a crossroads to me was just a matter of course to my parents. I'd been solo-traveling around the world for years. I've always been good at being alone. This was partly out of necessity, seeing as how I didn't have many friends growing up. I never clicked with the other kids in our town, and my classmates all lived an hour bus ride away, in the town of Barendrecht. I liked spending my free time inline skating or cycling—not on a cool, fast road bike, but just on my plain old Gazelle Trendy city bike. While my peers were sneaking out to secret barn parties and experimenting with makeup, boyfriends, and alcohol, my kind of fun was cycling 10 miles through the countryside on my own.

I blew on the hot mug of tea I was holding, creating small ripples on the surface.

"I just think I should take advantage of the situation," I concluded. "I haven't had this kind of opportunity in a while."

My relationship had ended, and underneath all the tears, I was also overcome by a powerful sense of freedom. Anything was possible again. The world was literally at my feet, and I could do whatever and go wherever I wanted. I could go live in Argentina, I thought. Or start a bed-and-breakfast in Ecuador. Or better yet, I could go traveling through Central Asia. That had been high up on my list for years. And now nothing and nobody was holding me back.

I looked at my parents and started to list a few more arguments, until I realized that they didn't need convincing.

–

The head of my department at work was a little less understanding the next day when I went into his office holding my resignation letter. I'd been working for a dredging company—quite literally standing knee-deep in mud—for years, first as a geologist and later as a superintendent on their ships. I had only been in my boss's office a handful of times before. Hidde was usually the one calling me at the crack of dawn on a Saturday, letting me know I'd be flying off to some faraway place like Uruguay that same evening to run a new harbor project. The only acceptable answer in those moments was: "Give me an hour and I'll be on my way to the airport." That's exactly how my job had started there five years earlier.

I had been hired by the company's geology department (which was, at the time, still unceremoniously referred to as the "ground department") on a Friday afternoon, and by Sunday morning I was on a plane to Indonesia for my very first project, my heart pounding. I was put on a small boat equipped with a wide variety of seismic instruments and tasked with finding offshore sand—mineable, coarse sand found on top of the seafloor. Each year, fifty billion tons of sand is used worldwide to manufacture cement, concrete, roads, glass, and even computer chips. There was no demand for oil or diamonds here, but there was plenty for sand, known to some as "new gold."

I would receive many more of those phone calls in the years following that first job in Indonesia and I loved it. It felt like I was being deployed on a secret mission of the highest urgency.

"Noraly, we need you *right now*. They're waiting for you in Panama."

To be fair, there were five people on the geology team, so four others could have taken my place, but still. I knew right from the start that I was made for this job. And now I was sitting in Hidde's office to let him know I was leaving—effective immediately.

"But you're already abroad for us all the time," Hidde said, sounding mildly insulted.

"I know, but that's different. I want to travel full time." I decided not to throw my immediate superior, Martin, under the bus; I didn't mention that my decision to quit had a lot to do with his telling me I might have to start working full time in the Netherlands.

"I wish I could understand, but I don't," he said, and I believed him.

"Luckily you don't have to," I replied.

"That's right," he said, adding that I was always welcome to come back. Some part of me was reassured by this, even though I was confident I wouldn't. When I walk away from something, I don't look back. I had meticulously wrapped up the last project I'd worked on, and thanks to my leftover vacation days, I wouldn't need to come in during my notice period.

My heart was pounding again and I had butterflies in my stomach, only this time I wasn't on a plane to Indonesia, but driving away from my old head office in Rotterdam.

–

A few days later, my cousin Laura dropped me off at the train station in what was now *her* small Kia. I didn't want some big, dramatic goodbye—I've always hated those. I prefer a quiet exit where I don't have to see how much my departures hurt the people I am leaving behind. I was wearing my big black backpack on my back, a smaller dark green daypack on my stomach, and a pair of cheap sunglasses on my nose. I quickly took off the daypack, put it down, and gave my cousin a hug. We held each other tightly and she whispered: "Have an amazing time."

I looked at her and nodded. "Thank you. Enjoy your new car, and your freedom!"

I grinned and put the daypack back on. Everything I'd have with me for the foreseeable future had been reduced to what I could carry on my body. All my other worldly possessions, those I hadn't sold or given away, were neatly stashed in a storage unit in Utrecht. I had no idea when I would see them again or what I would do with them when I did. I gave Laura a final wave and walked to my platform.

I stared at the two plane tickets in my hand while I waited for my train to arrive. I had a connection in Abu Dhabi, which had been cheaper than booking a direct flight to India. My first trip to India eight years ago had dramatically changed my life. Now that I was at another important crossroads, it felt right to go back there. India was apparently the place where all my big life changes took place. The first time I went backpacking there, in 2010, I sat down in an internet café in northern India to send an important email. I wrote a message to my organic geochemistry professor at the University of Utrecht, where I'd received my master's degree, and told him that I wouldn't be returning to start a PhD. In doing so, I was ending my academic career before it had even begun. Instead, I somehow ended up in Australia, where I found a job as a geologist, working in gold exploration. Now, eight years later, I'd left my career as superintendent behind and was returning to India. This time, I had a new ambition: I was going to make a name for myself as a travel blogger.

I had chosen Leh, a town in northern India, as my starting point. I'd never been there, but I'd heard that it was a good hub for trekking through the Himalayas. A few weeks of hiking seemed like the ideal way to plan my next move now that I'd quit my job.

To become a travel blogger—that's as far as I got. I wasn't exactly sure how to become one, or for that matter what I'd write about. I wasn't too worried about all that yet though—even if nothing worth writing about happened on this hike, I would at least have an amazing time in the wilderness.

In Leh, I joined an organized trekking tour accompanied by a guide and packhorses, and a week later we reached Tso Moriri, a bright blue mountain lake at an altitude of almost fifteen thousand feet. The guided trek ended there, but I'd gotten a taste for it and wanted to continue hiking to the next valley over: Spiti Valley. I didn't have my own tent or camping gear, let alone any idea of what route to take, so going alone was not an option. There was a village on the lake, Karzok, where I stayed for a few days to look for travel companions. After asking around for some time, I eventually met two Indian guys on their way to Spiti who were passing through with their little pack donkeys. I joined them and was allowed to sleep in their tent on the donkey's blankets, and together we hiked across glaciers and over 16,500-foot-tall mountains, reaching our destination in four days. The journey had exhausted me physically, but I found myself brimming with energy, mentally. I took a shared cab to Manali, a town in the Indian state of Himachal Pradesh, where I took a few days to catch up on sleep and recover from the hardship. There, I started my first blog post.

In between writing sessions, I took short walks through the village in an attempt to soothe my muscles, which were still sore from the trek. I climbed up the stairs to Rasta Café, my usual place, and sat down on a cushion on the floor at one of the low tables. I had come to know the menu by heart and immediately ordered a Veg Delight sandwich and a chai. I'd hoped to find some backpackers who I could join for my meal, but when I glanced around me I only saw a couple sitting at one of the other tables. *Shame*, I thought, I wouldn't have minded a bit of conversation. While I waited for my order, a handsome young man with light brown eyes and thick black hair down to his shoulders walked by.

"How are you?" he asked when he saw me looking at him.

"Good, you?" I responded. "Do you work here?"

"No." He laughed. "But I do work downstairs, in the motorcycle shop. I'm Pankaj."

I'd noticed a number of Royal Enfield motorcycles at the shop below, but I hadn't paid them much mind.

"That's so cool. Do you sell them?"

"No, I rent them out. I also organize guided motorcycle tours," he added.

"I ride too," I began to say, but he seemed in a hurry to leave and my words were left unanswered in the air. Once I'd finished my tea and my sandwich, I paid and walked downstairs. I stuck my head around the doorway of Pankaj's store and shouted: "Bye, see you later!"

"Come in, come in," he said enthusiastically when he saw me. "Didn't you say you ride motorcycles? Go ahead and try sit on one of these." So he *had* heard me.

He pointed at the bikes in the back and said: "We have a few Royal Enfield Bullets, you know, real classics. But we usually go for these, the *Hima-lyans.* That's Royal Enfield's proper off-road motorcycle."

I noticed that he pronounced *Himalayan* differently than I did, but after hearing it a few more times I became convinced that his was the way it was supposed to be said. I obediently repeated the word Hima-lyan long enough until it felt natural. The classic bikes in the back were not really my thing, but I did like the look of these Hima-lyans.

"How much would it be to rent one of those?" I asked casually.

"For you, twelve hundred rupees per day."

I laughed. "Special price for me, right?"

I did some quick math to figure out how much it was and realized that twelve hundred rupees was only sixteen dollars a day. Dirt cheap. I wondered if this might be the solution to a problem that had arisen just that morning. I had messaged my best friend, Mandy, who had trekked through the Zanskar Valley in the Kargil District years ago. For years I'd desperately wanted to go see it for myself after hearing her incredible stories. It was apparently home to some impressive Buddhist temples and its location between tall mountain ridges was said to be stunning. The valley was cut off from the outside world for six months every year due to heavy snowfall in the mountain passes, so timing was of the essence.

"I'm in Manali right now," I'd messaged Mandy. "I'm just not sure how to get to Zanskar, but if I manage to get there I want to go to Kashmir after."

"Could I get to Zanskar by motorcycle?" I asked myself aloud.

"Yes, absolutely," Pankaj replied, as if I had directed my question at him. "And this is the right moment," he said, alluding to the approaching snowy season. "If you want to see Zanskar this year, now is the time," he said encouragingly. I looked from Pankaj to the motorcycles and then back.

"You do really know how to ride, right?" he asked, suddenly suspicious.

"Yes, of course I know how to ride."

My reply came out sharper than I had intended, but I'd had my license for three years at that point and had done well over 6,000 miles through the Netherlands on my Ducati Monster 796. I'd fallen in love with motorcycling from the very first lesson. From then on, it was my favorite thing to do in the world. I had gone to the Ducati dealership to buy my first bike—a secondhand Monster—the very same day I got my license.

A 796 isn't known as a beginner's bike because it's not. It's completely unmanageable in the hands of a novice, especially mine. At low RPMs, the bike bucked more violently than a mechanical bull and I clung to the handlebars like my life depended on it. But the sound coming out of the dual Akrapovič exhaust and the glossy red paint of the tank evaporated all my fears. As long as the road looked reasonably dry, I'd be out for a ride. I didn't have any friends who rode and never picked a destination. I often spent hours riding around aimlessly, and taking my Ducati for a spin was the first thing I did when I came back from working abroad.

Now, three years later, I had the bucking under control, and my riding skills were pretty decent. What I didn't know was that experience on a city bike, like my Monster, was completely irrelevant for the journey I was about to embark on. And even if I had known, I'm not sure I would have wanted to admit it.

—

I walked into Pankaj's shop early the next morning, wriggled out of the shoulder straps of my backpack and put it down. I hadn't wasted any time and had started making preparations for my trip to Zanskar immediately after our previous conversation. He'd promised me I could borrow a helmet and gloves from him but everything else I'd have to arrange myself. Proper motorcycle gear like I wore in the Netherlands was nowhere to be found around there, so I bought a secondhand man's leather jacket, short leather boots, and cheap-looking knee protectors. I ran out of time to plan a route, but figured I would get around to that later. The general idea was to ride back to Leh first, then come up with the best route to Zanskar. I told Pankaj I would rent the bike for three weeks; that end date would be my only obligation. I had checked out from my hostel and with all my belongings stuffed into my backpack, all I needed now was the motorcycle. Pretty simple actually, I thought.

Pankaj beckoned me and pointed proudly at the white Hima-lyan he had readied for me. On the back, a steel rack had been welded to each side of the motorcycle.

"Here," he said. "I got two extra jerrycans for you, they'll fit in here."

He demonstrated how the jerrycans fit into the racks. "You'll need them for Zanskar. Don't forget you can only get gas in Padum and nowhere else," he stressed.

I nodded, but I barely heard a word he said. I only had eyes for the bike. My heart skipped a beat and told me resolutely: that's the one I want. Pankaj and I circled around the white Royal Enfield together.

"Everything is in perfect order, I serviced it and everything," he said. He gave the rear tire a gentle kick. "Brand-new."

I was about to say something approving when I spotted a tear. In the swingarm, no less.

"Look at that," I exclaimed, pointing at the pivoting arm that connects the rear wheel to the frame of the motorcycle. "That's not right."

Pankaj stared at it bewildered and turned quiet. I kneeled next to the motorcycle and carefully ran my finger along the tear. With my eyes wide open, I daydreamed about what could have happened if I had taken this bike on the road. In my imagination, the entire swingarm broke off, sending me and half a motorcycle plummeting into a ravine. Or the rear wheel popped off, rolling along the road next to me. I watched myself go over the handlebars and somersault a dozen times before sliding my head over the asphalt.

"I'll repair it," said Pankaj, abruptly pulling me out of my homemade horror movie.

"Okay, great," I mumbled, wondering how on earth the swingarm could have gotten torn in the first place.

–

While Pankaj was busy producing a new swingarm from somewhere, I walked to a travel agency office, a little farther down the road. I had found out the night before that I needed a permit to cross the Rohtang

Pass, which had caused me a small panic. The mountain pass sat at about thirteen thousand feet in altitude and connected the Kullu Valley to the Lahaul and Spiti valleys. It was the only way to get to Leh, and I hadn't considered that I might need special permission to cross it. The travel agent gave me a surprised look when I asked for a one-way ticket to the Rohtang Pass.

"Today? You're going by bike? Alone?" he repeated to make sure he'd heard me right. I nodded. "That will be very difficult," he said gravely. "People book this weeks in advance. Not on the day of departure." He paused, seemingly for dramatic effect, and I already knew this would cost me. The game of negotiation and haggling amused me at times, but usually I didn't feel like playing, let alone make time for it. I asked how much this was going to cost me, already riffling through the stack of bills in my hand.

"Six hundred fifty rupees," he said curtly from behind his computer screen. I peeled the required bills adorned with Mahatma Gandhi's face off the stack and handed them over. An hour later, I stepped outside with my printed permit and hurried back to Pankaj. I found him squatting next to the bike, holding a new swingarm in his hands.

When he saw me, he looked up and said: "It's going to be fine, I'm almost done!"

Thirty minutes later the bike was ready, and Pankaj again assured me everything was shipshape. I tied my backpack onto the back of the motorcycle. I wouldn't make it all the way to Leh before the end of the day, but I wasn't planning to do so anyway. Leh was 267 miles away, and that seemed way too far to ride in one day. As long as I made it past the Rohtang Pass, I'd be able to spend the night in Darcha, a town about 63 miles from Manali. I swung my leg over the seat, grabbed the handlebar, and started the engine. Pankaj waved me off from his doorway, enthusiastically calling after me: "See you in three weeks!"

"Yeah, see you then," I yelled back, trying to pull away as smoothly as possible. This was only the third motorcycle I'd ever ridden. Other than my learner bike and my Ducati Monster, I had zero experience with other models. My position on the Himalayan was a lot higher thanks to its large front wheel, but luckily there was no sign of the Monster's uncontrollable character. I got through the first corner without issue and breathed a sigh of relief. I was on my way!

–

I set out toward the Rohtang Pass, following the main road until Palchan. There, I turned onto a smaller road that started to climb almost immediately, snaking up the tree-covered mountainside. I was glad it was still paved, giving me plenty of time to get used to the bike. The smell from the pine trees was so strong that I closed my helmet's visor to shut it out. I already regretted borrowing a helmet from Pankaj. It didn't fit me one bit, and I wondered if this was because of my head's shape or the helmet's. While I pondered the contours of my cranium, a checkpoint suddenly materialized ahead. I hadn't noticed quite how much altitude I'd gained; I'd ridden straight into a low-hanging cloud. I slowed down and came to a stop next to a man in uniform with a raised hand.

"Permit," was all he said.

"Just a moment please," I replied, unfolding my kickstand with my left foot and somewhat clumsily dismounting the bike. I had neatly tucked away my permit in my backpack, but that meant it was now buried under all my luggage. When I finally and triumphantly produced the piece of paper, the man pointed at a small booth nearby.

"Show it there," he barked. I didn't even manage three steps in the direction of the booth when my motorcycle came down with a racket. I spun around, looking at the man in uniform in alarm. "Sorry, sorry," I mumbled, and started hauling the bike as quickly as I could to get it back upright. The driver behind me had already jumped out of his car to help me, and together with the man in uniform we got the whole mess upright. To my surprise, I couldn't spot a single scratch. I was convinced that if I'd dropped my Ducati like that, the resulting damage would have cost me hundreds. Thank goodness the Royal Enfield resembled a tank more than anything else. I felt myself relax.

Once my permit had been checked, I was waved through. I carried on riding until I'd reached the Rohtang Pass. Multiple cars were parked along the side of the road, and Indian tourists were taking pictures with the sign announcing the altitude. The cloud I'd entered just before the checkpoint hadn't dissipated, and I was already freezing cold. Without a view to admire and with my hands shaking, I decided to just keep going.

Until now, the road had been smooth asphalt, but on the other side of the pass it continued unpaved, descending steeply down the mountainside. I had zero experience with unpaved roads, so what better way to start gaining some than with the infamous Rohtang Pass. What started as an easy-to-navigate gravel path quickly turned into a rocky road along a dizzying cliff edge.

"Oh no, oh no," I said out loud as I bounced uncontrollably down the mountain. I had no idea how to control my descent when the road basically consisted of big rocks. I desperately pulled my front brake, messed around with the clutch, and slammed the rear brake at random intervals. While crossing a rivulet of meltwater that ran down the mountainside and over the path, my front wheel hit a boulder and I crashed. I came down so hard that it knocked all the air out of my lungs. I gingerly got to my feet and didn't move for a few seconds while I assessed whether I'd hurt myself. I looked at the bike. One of the jerrycans was almost submerged, so I quickly took it out of the side rack so the water wouldn't seep into it. Having secured the jerrycan, I focused on the crashed motorcycle. I thought lifting it would be a piece of cake—after all, it had taken no time at all at the checkpoint. I had conveniently forgotten that two men had helped me then. My muscles groaned and my face turned red from the effort. It felt like I was trying to lift a sleeping rhino. The bike refused to yield and stubbornly stayed exactly where it was. It was probably for the best that I didn't know then how often this would happen to me, how much time I would soon spend despondently looking at a motorcycle lying upside down on the ground. If I had known, I might have quit then and there.

I looked around. There had been plenty of people up on the pass, but on this side of the mountain there was no one in sight. There was no other way around it; I would have to address the situation on my own. I changed tactics and grabbed the bike's metal rack with my left hand and the handlebar with my right. I bent my knees slightly and started to push, using the boulders as leverage. Encouraged by some slight movement, I pushed and pushed until the bike was back upright.

"Yes!" I exclaimed over the valley, pleased with myself. I placed the jerrycan back in the rack, and while balancing the bike with one hand, I carefully got back on the seat and continued my bouncing descent. I reached Darcha by the end of the afternoon without any further tumbles. I found a place to spend the night at a guesthouse called the

Buddha Homestay. Less than half an hour after dragging my backpack into the room, I heard a number of motorcycles approaching. I took a few quick steps over to the window and pulled back the curtain. Four motorcyclists and a car were parking next to my bike. I joined their group for dinner that evening.

They were British, as it turned out. They sat at a long, low table, paint peeling along its edges. Lively discussions about the pros and cons of hard aluminum cases versus soft luggage bags, tubed or tubeless tires, and the best tire profile for this terrain were the talk of the evening. I sat at the end of the table, and for a while I tried to nod at the right moments or laugh strategically, to hide the fact that I had nothing to add to the conversation. Eventually I skulked off, feeling like even more of an idiot than I had earlier that day when I'd hurtled down the mountain. I was angry at myself for not asking Pankaj more questions, or perhaps taking an off-road motorcycling course before setting off. Starting this journey on a whim because it seemed like a convenient way to reach Zanskar suddenly didn't feel like such a good idea anymore. But it didn't occur to me to give up or turn around. I had started this so I would finish it too, scared and clueless if I had to. I had been raised with a "less talking, more doing" mentality, but in this case asking a few questions first might have been useful.

–

The next morning, I woke up in the mustiness of a room without enough airflow and took a quick shower. The water was cold. I dried myself with the towel that I'd found folded on my bed the previous night and pulled on my motorcycle pants. I tied on the knee protectors, which were held in place with Velcro, and squeezed into my boots. When I looked outside, I saw that the group of motorcyclists and their support car from yesterday had already disappeared. They were on a tight schedule and didn't have any time to lose. I was secretly relieved they'd left, so I could get ready in my own time without being asked technical questions that I couldn't answer. It was a chilly morning, and I quickly zipped up my leather jacket. It took some messing with the bungee cords, but finally my backpack was secured on the bike again and I pulled away.

It took me all day to reach Leh, but the road was good and apart from a few sections with construction, everything thankfully went well. It felt strange to be back in Leh, having landed there only three weeks earlier, but it was also nice to be in familiar surroundings, especially now that everything around motorcycling felt so unknown and uncertain. I was disappointed that I couldn't stay in the same hotel as I had before, but it was only accessible via a footpath with stairs, and I didn't want to just abandon my bike somewhere down the street. I thought about Pankaj, who had instructed me to take good care of the bike and have it serviced regularly. I had traveled 267 miles by this point and wondered if anything had to be done on the bike already. I wasn't in the mood to feel foolish again and decided not to ask Pankaj. A bit of extra maintenance never hurts, I thought. With that in mind I made my way to a Royal Enfield workshop I'd seen on my way to the hotel.

"You're lucky you came here, miss," said the salesman. "We employ the very best, longest-serving mechanic in all of Leh." He grinned so widely that his mustache curled up far enough to touch his cheeks.

It was true that their mechanic looked like he had personally experienced the evolution of motorcycles. I didn't need an appointment; he started working on my bike right away. He appeared a little fragile, but his steadfastness told me he knew what he was doing. I spied on him out of the corner of my eye. With any luck, I might learn something and potentially be able to do any further maintenance on the bike myself, I thought. The mechanic started by unscrewing the air filter's protective cover. Although, I only realized that's where the air filter lived once he took it out and held it up. I'd never seen a motorcycle's air filter before, let alone a dirty one, so I didn't know what it was supposed to look like. Given the look on the mechanic's face, it was far from fabulous. He shook his head at me.

"This is not good. Not good."

He turned the key, started the bike and held the filter in front of the exhaust while his assistant revved the engine—which is apparently how you clean an air filter. The dust cloud that emerged was so large that I broke out into a coughing fit. According to the mechanic, the air filter hadn't been cleaned for thousands of miles and I started to doubt Pankaj's optimistic assurances about the bike being "shipshape." I didn't know enough about motorcycles to specifically tell the mechanic what else to check though. For the past three years, I'd just dropped off my Ducati Monster at the dealership in the Netherlands whenever it needed to be serviced. I didn't have the slightest idea what they did to it, or what parts needed to be cleaned or replaced when. And I knew even less about the maintenance of off-road motorcycles. I opted for a general request.

"Could you check everything?"

The mechanic blinked. "Everything?"

"Well, you know, the most important things," I said as nonchalantly as possible. He nodded slightly and then said: "Come back in a couple of hours and it'll be ready." I did, not realizing until I returned that I still didn't know what they'd done, or what had been due for servicing. I never let anyone wrench on my bike in my absence ever again.

With a motorcycle that was now hopefully in good condition, I explored Ladakh some more, before eventually setting course for the Zanskar Valley. The condition of the road changed constantly. Sometimes it was gravel or even big rocks I had to dodge, sometimes the road was so broken up that it was more pothole than anything else, and then it would be back to smooth asphalt. The latter didn't require as much focus, and my thoughts would start to wander.

Like a magnet, they kept being pulled back to the end of my relationship. I was riding through spectacular scenery and dramatic views, but I didn't see any of it. It was like my eyes were fixed on the road, but my pupils were turned inward. I had expected to feel euphoric and supremely free on this ride, like I had felt so strongly on my previous solo travels. Instead, there were moments of such profound heartbreak that I felt like ripping out my heart with my bare hands. Maybe I should have gone even farther away, put even more oceans and continents between us so I would stop thinking about him. But I doubted that would have helped. I tumbled back in time.

–

Just six months earlier, I was crying uncontrollably in the arms of my neighbor, in front of our house, in the middle of the street. My heart-wrenching sobs had sounded like the cries of a wounded animal. I didn't know I could cry like that. It was the day after I'd finally brought to light the raw, inevitable truth. My tears came like a warm tidal wave, and I cried for days. I cried over the betrayal, the lies, the future there no longer was, and the love that had apparently never been there in the first place. I cried until I had no tears left, no matter how hard I tried. He had begged me not to end the relationship. "You did nothing wrong," he'd said. But that was so unsatisfying that I didn't even know what I was supposed to do with it. This must be my fault too, somehow.

What had I done wrong? I had to know. No matter how hard or how long I thought about it, I couldn't figure it out. My head was like a hamster wheel, my thoughts the hamster that runs and runs and never gets anywhere. I was driving myself bonkers.

These were the questions I asked myself over and over on my way to Zanskar, singing "Skin" by Rag'n'Bone Man and crying into my helmet.

We had both been in my therapist's office a week after I'd discovered the truth, the same professional I had seen for months after I got burned-out from work the previous year. I sat in the blue velvet swivel chair, my usual spot for our weekly sessions. I got to pick my seat beforehand. My partner would have to take the couch; it was less comfortable.

"Why? Why?" I asked, my words hanging heavy in the air. That was the question that was consuming me. I just didn't get it.

"I don't know, I really don't know," he whined desperately from the couch. Even after the endless lies he'd told me, I believed him. I believed that he really didn't know why he'd been having an affair for almost six months. With a coworker who was fourteen years older than the both of us, no less.

"I didn't realize how incredibly lucky I was to have you until now." He was crying. I looked away, worried the sight of his sadness might convince me to change my mind. When I'd found out about his affair, I'd screamed at him over the phone to not even think about coming home. He would just have to stay with *her*. But he hadn't done that and had been staying for weeks with his parents instead.

He was hoping I'd let him come back because I'd left the door ajar; I hadn't immediately put an end to the relationship. The end of our relationship meant I could lose my house. It would mean my in-laws, whom I adored, wouldn't be a part of my life anymore. It would mean saying goodbye to the future I had envisioned with him. I wasn't ready to do that yet. I felt like I was walking on a tightrope over an emotional abyss, trying desperately to keep my balance on the thin cord and make it to the other side.

While he was at his parents', I went back to work, which was in Buenos Aires. My boss had sent me out there on a new project, and it gave me the space I needed to weigh up whether I wanted to stay with him or not. The stress and heartbreak made me shed weight like water and after my six-week rotation I returned to the Netherlands, skinny.

"I can't stay with you," I eventually said quietly from the blue velvet chair. I felt empty and numb. Then my voice broke. "And I resent you for making me end it. For putting that on me. I didn't choose this."

Anger and sorrow were fighting for dominance, and I gave in to anger. As long as I was angry, I was shielded from my sadness. I couldn't keep that up for long, though. With that one simple sentence, I was alone again—and soon to be homeless on top of that. At least, that's how it felt. Obviously I didn't really have to be homeless. I had family and wonderful friends who would let me stay with them. I could apply for a new mortgage, try to buy another place. But anything I could afford on my own would be a serious step down from my current house, and that felt like a failure. I had always progressed to better things; I'd never gone back to something that had already been.

My first place after moving out of my parents' house was a sixty-five square foot room. It was in an abandoned building on the grounds of Altrecht in Den Dolder. Altrecht was a facility that specialized in the treatment of people with severe psychiatric illnesses and personality disorders—not an ideal place for an eighteen-year-old student, but the only room I could afford near Utrecht, where I went to university. A few months later I was able to sign up for student accommodation and moved to Zeist, which was a bit closer to Utrecht. This time I had ten other students as housemates. We shared a toilet, a shower, and a kitchen. My room was more than twice the size of my previous one— a very respectable 161 square feet. After numerous moves in the years that followed, involving scores more landlords, housemates, and shared bathrooms, I bought my first apartment in Utrecht. I sold it barely a year later so I could live together with the love of my life, in what I thought would be the final stop on this home journey: a spacious semidetached house with a garden bordering on a forest.

I didn't want to lose this dream home, but it happened anyway. The bank decided I couldn't pay my mortgage on my own, even though

I knew I could. The only way I'd be able to keep the house was by submitting a letter from my employer detailing my salary, including my international allowances. But despite having worked abroad almost exclusively for nearly five years, my supervisor refused to provide it. "That's company policy," I was told. "It's the base salary that matters. We can't guarantee the international allowances."

"I know that. But this letter doesn't make you my guarantors, and the bank can't force you to give me anything," I countered. "What's important is that the bank can see what my actual salary is, and that it's enough for me to pay the mortgage on my own."

"I'm sure, but we're really not doing it," I was told.

I swallowed. "Then I'll lose my house." I allowed my words to sink in for a moment.

No reaction.

"Can you at least send me abroad as a permanent expat for a few years so I won't be out on the street here in the Netherlands?" I asked, my voice trembling lightly. The company had dozens of permanent expats working abroad, and I knew that these positions came with accommodation included.

But I was told that might not be possible. "In fact, we've just got a new project in the Netherlands. I might just put you on that and not send you abroad at all for the coming year."

I couldn't believe what I was hearing. How had this conversation turned so quickly from what I'd wanted—and so badly needed—to the complete opposite? Were they simply trying to prove a point that they couldn't guarantee international allowances? Whatever the reason, it became clear that arguing wouldn't get me anywhere. My throat had grown so tight with anxiety that I couldn't get out another word anyway.

I walked out of the office with my head held high, but my legs felt like lead. Now I knew for sure: I would lose my house and have to find a new place to live in the Netherlands sooner rather than later. But I didn't want to go back to some city apartment in a bad neighborhood, or a room on the grounds of an asylum. I'd rather have no home at all.

–

The only thing that could pull me out of hours-long sessions of melo-dramatic self-pity and melancholy, back into the here and now, was unpaved roads. On the treacherous roads of Ladakh, I didn't have time to play the feature-length movie about my house of cards collapsing for the thousandth time. My shoulders tensed in an effort to keep my front wheel straight while it tried to break to the side every time it hit a rock. My eyes feverishly scanned the path, looking far away, nearby, far away, nearby. Choosing the right lines turned out to be an art, one I sometimes thought I'd mastered but often completely missed the mark. I couldn't brood or torture myself while riding off-road. The unpaved road had become my new obsession.

When I finally entered the Zanskar Valley, I knew Mandy had been right. Surrounded by mountains, I rode past fields of flowers, turquoise rivers, and tiny villages with white cottages. From a distance they looked just like sugar cubes. I saw herds of yaks, the long-haired cattle with large horns that were kept here, and multiple groundhogs scurrying toward their burrows. Wolves and snow leopards were native to the area too, but though they may have seen me, I never saw them. Every view was a piece of art. Zanskar was so overwhelmingly beautiful that I didn't feel my constant hunger or thirst, the freezing cold, or my painful behind from the hours I'd spent on the seat of the motorcycle.

A few days later, I'd reached the city Srinagar in Kashmir. I booked a room in a houseboat on Dal Lake and met its owner: Hamid, aka "Uncle." Hamid immediately made me feel a part of the family and he invited me as his guest to his niece Inshah's wedding. It was an invitation I couldn't decline. I promised him I would come back a few weeks later for the wedding and rode back to Manali to return my rental bike.

I had ridden more than 1,800 miles in three weeks' time, surviving my baptism by fire as a motorcycle adventurer. Pankaj looked both surprised and relieved when I rolled into his shop on a bike that was still fully intact. I was glad to have returned to Manali in one piece too, but when I walked through the streets soon after, my backpack back on my shoulders instead of strapped to my motorcycle, I felt oddly displaced. It was as though I'd parked not a motorcycle but my freedom in Pankaj's shop. Did I really have to go back to squeezing myself into a ramshackle bus, which, spurred on by deafening Punjabi rap music, torpedoed itself around bends with screeching brakes while I held somebody's chicken on my lap? I had traveled the world for years like that without a peep, using all possible modes of public transport. Now, just the idea of it made me feel sick. I hadn't expected to become attached to having my own transportation so quickly and fiercely.

I didn't have much time to grieve the loss of my rental bike, though. I had a flight booked for Bangladesh. There were three weeks until Inshah's wedding in Kashmir, and I'd decided to spend that time exploring a new country. Bangladesh was another place Mandy had told me a lot about, and it seemed like a fantastic country to write a few articles for my travel blog. I'd written multiple articles about Ladakh, Zanskar, and Kashmir on my motorcycle journey, though they'd been read by only a handful of people. Perhaps Bangladesh would speak more to the readers' imaginations? After arriving in the capital city, Dhaka, I took buses to every corner of the country and frantically wrote about everything there was to do and see. Though it felt like mere days since I'd announced I was going to be a travel blogger, it seemed as though that particular career path hit the rocks before I could say "travel blogger." Nobody gave a hoot about my stories, and I wasn't earning a single cent. Every time I checked my bank account, I watched with a sinking feeling how my money was disappearing, with absolutely nothing coming back in. I'd always earned a good living at the dredging company, especially with those additional allowances I received when working in countries that had been labeled as "dangerous" or "who else would be crazy enough to go here?" I'd been able to save a lot while working in Brazil (category 1) and Kazakhstan (category 2). I also had a good bit of home equity after the sale of my house, which was funding me so far. But I'd have to find another way to make money, or this adventure would come to an end sooner than I'd like. I wanted to avoid at all costs having to crawl back to Hidde for a job. Or, worse, to Martin.

I flew from Bangladesh back to India for Inshah's wedding in Kashmir. And just like the two times I'd been there prior, a visit to India somehow proved synonymous with a change in my path. Until Irfan approached me at the wedding, I'd been struggling to figure out what to do with my life, now that being a travel blogger didn't amount to anything.

It wasn't until after the wedding, when I was standing in Delhi and Irfan handed me the keys to Basanti, that I realized that what I'd actually bought from him was freedom. I was no longer dependent on bus routes to choose my destinations for me. And once I had decided to ride my new motorcycle to Kuala Lumpur, I was suddenly struck with a solution to both my writing and my liquidity problem. A motorcycle trip was much more suited to moving pictures than the written word, I thought. I would keep writing, but I suspected it might be easier to find an audience for my journeys—and make money in the process—by posting videos. I opened a YouTube account, watched instructional videos about video editing for a week, and bought myself an action camera. My very first video was of a ride on Basanti through the city center of Delhi, accompanied by obnoxious music that in hindsight was far too loud. The video was only two minutes long and incredibly bad, but my YouTube channel Itchy Boots was born.

Chapter 3

A Ridiculous Plan

Miles: 0

I handed my camera to the manager of Hotel Cosmo and told him what to do.

"Here, push this button and film me while I ride away on my bike," I said. He nodded earnestly. He got into position across the road and gave me a thumbs-up.

"Okay, now!" I shouted and rode a few feet out onto the street. Then I stopped, waited for him to bring me the camera and screwed it onto my helmet. I remember thinking: *If this is what I need to do every time, this trip is going to take a while.* Then I gratefully shook his hand and said goodbye.

"Always welcome here," he said with a wide smile.

"If I'm ever back in Delhi, I'll stay with you again," I promised.

I kicked Basanti into first gear, revved my engine and didn't look back. From then on, my eyes were fixed on the road ahead, with Kuala Lumpur, Malaysia, as my first destination. I rode toward Mathura, a small town between Delhi and Agra. I had visited the world-famous Taj Mahal in Agra on my first trip to India, so this time I'd decided to visit Mathura, one of the seven holy cities for Hindus and traditionally said to be the birthplace of the god Krishna. I forged a path through the busy traffic of Delhi. Rickshaws, the characteristic three-wheeled mopeds with a passenger cabin, were everywhere but there were also regular mopeds, buses spewing black exhaust fumes, cyclists, ox wagons, and handcarts. Small groups of cows meandered between the vehicles or lay sleeping in the middle of the road. But I didn't mind the busy traffic—I was far too excited about the prospect of the long trip ahead.

I rode straight through the state of Uttar Pradesh toward the border with Myanmar. This time around, I didn't have much time to travel at a leisurely pace through India. Myanmar's regulations were to blame for that. The government required tourists to hire a local guide so they could keep an eye on the foreigners in their country, which meant I had to be at the Myanmar border on a set date to join a group.

Delhi may have had the reputation of being the most polluted city in India, but the smog was just as unbearable in cities like Lucknow, Varanasi, and Patna. The steel-gray sky, sometimes backlit by a dim yellow-and-pink sun, was stifling. I was so desperate for fresh air that I decided to take a brief detour to Sikkim. Wedged between China, Nepal, and Bhutan, high up in the mountains, Sikkim is the most sparsely populated state in India. I couldn't imagine the smog would linger there. The mountain village Darjeeling was located just outside of Sikkim, and as this was the only town in the area I'd heard of, I typed in "darjeeling" on my phone. It was a 265-mile ride away, which according to Google Maps would take me eleven hours. I had never traveled that far in one day before, let alone sat on my bike for that long. I had no idea if I could do it. But the next morning, when I stepped out of the small wooden chalet where I'd spent the night and saw the dirty gray sky, I decided that I could. I quickly hauled my backpack outside and tied it onto the back of my motorcycle. I'd become quite handy with the bungee cords, and it took me less and less time to get ready each morning. I started Basanti, glanced at the eleven-hour-and-one-minute travel time on my screen, and sped off.

The first few miles I rode that day were through the ugliest part of India that I'd ever seen. Small trash fires burned everywhere you looked on the side of the road. The smell of burning plastic was even worse than that of the smog, and every time I passed a fire I involuntarily held my breath. I passed landfills with gaunt, sick cows eating trash, and little kids poking around in it. The houses were patchworks of plastic, cloth, and pieces of wood, and even from the road I could see that most of them were on the verge of collapse. Young women—barely more than children themselves—walked to and fro with bags of construction debris balanced on their heads, dressed in gorgeous, colorful saris. Their elaborate, graceful garments contrasted sharply with their dull, tired eyes. The women were the ones doing this heavy manual labor, and a sense of both pride and sorrow welled up inside me. I had always seen

India as a country of ungraspable juxtapositions, and this experience was no exception. I remembered the Kashmiri wedding—the abundance of food, the expensive clothes, all the gifts—and then looked at groups of people sitting around burned trash, skinny and without possessions.

I kept a steady pace and only stopped briefly to have some chai or stretch my legs. The seat was so uncomfortable that my glutes, back, and shoulders first started aching and then stiffened up completely. The only thing that kept me going was that the air pollution was noticeably decreasing. At first, I started seeing patches of blue peeking through the gray blanket of sky, but eventually the smog disappeared completely and the sun appeared. The first mountains emerged in the distance, and I subconsciously picked up a bit of speed. Then the road started to wind and climb. I was so focused on getting through the bends, on avoiding the dogs crossing the road and other road users pulling weird stunts, that I didn't even notice how the miles flew by. Before I knew it I only had 31 miles left to Darjeeling. I stopped at a gas station to fuel up.

I attracted a lot of attention whenever I stopped somewhere, and this time was no different. When I took off my helmet and it became clear that I was a blond, foreign woman, a crowd would appear out of nowhere. It was like everyone dropped whatever they were doing to come look at me. I never understood where people came from so quickly. It was always men, and usually none of them said a word. They simply gathered around me in a circle and proceeded to stare at me in silence. I'd spent enough time in India to know that this was normal, so I didn't usually feel threatened. I never really got used to the intense stares though.

I paid the attendant and got back on my bike. While quickly trying to get away from the crowd, I had to make a sharp turn to get back onto the main road. I promptly released the clutch too fast, stalling the engine and dumping Basanti on the ground in the middle of the road. I felt my cheeks flush with embarrassment and couldn't bring myself to look back at the crowd of people who were still watching me. Thankfully, two of the men who had been staring came to my aid, and we righted the motorcycle together.

"Thanks, thanks," I mumbled, still embarrassed. I quickly squeezed the clutch lever and pressed the start button, but nothing happened. Nothing at all. I frowned and tried again—nothing again.

"Doesn't start?" one of the men asked.

"No," I replied, starting to panic. I was standing in the middle of a main road, and all of a sudden my motorcycle wouldn't start. I couldn't make sense of it. How could I have broken the starter motor? Was a minor drop really all it took?

"Here," said the man. He flipped Basanti's red kill switch, waited a few seconds, and flipped it back. "Try again."

I pushed the start button again, and to my utter amazement she started immediately. *Never knew motorcycles had reset buttons*, I thought, while hastily moving over to the side of the road. I gave the man who had helped me a thank-you wave and then quickly took off, my cheeks still flushed with shame.

It wasn't long before I had forgotten all about the incident and was completely absorbed by the spectacular mountains I was passing through. I whizzed over the asphalt, trying to take every turn a little faster, a little more smoothly and at a slightly sharper angle than the one before it. "You know, I'm already a pretty good rider," I mused aloud. The words had barely left my mouth when I suddenly came down. I was just exiting a bend when my rear wheel slipped right out from underneath me. I slid across the asphalt, bike and all, hearing nothing but the high scratching sound of my motorcycle scraping across the road surface. A bus coming from the other direction slammed its brakes, but neither of us could prevent me from sliding straight toward it. I couldn't tell if I scraped across the asphalt for ten seconds or ten minutes, but it felt like an eternity. I finally came to a stop just a few yards away from the bus, where I stayed motionless on the road. Several people immediately jumped out and hurried toward me.

"Are you okay? Are you okay?" they shouted, visibly shaken.

"Uh, yeah," I said, surprised that nothing hurt. Bewildered, I sat up and looked back. The right footpeg and my right pannier had drawn two long white lines across the asphalt. I hadn't even touched the road—my leg had been protected by my aluminum pannier. Apart from a few scratches, Basanti wasn't damaged either. The other passengers of the bus were hanging out of the windows by now to gain a better view of what was happening outside.

"Sorry, sorry," I said, raising my hand to the bus driver. I walked around Basanti and grabbed her handlebars. The passengers who had gotten off the bus helped, and together we pushed until she was back on her wheels. I involuntarily shook my head. After everything going fine for hours, I had spectacularly messed up twice on the last stretch. I was so grateful that bystanders hadn't hesitated to help me in both situations. I took a deep breath of fresh mountain air to compose myself, then calmly got back on my bike.

I was a lot more careful the rest of the way to Darjeeling. Twilight was tentatively creeping in when I turned into the city's steep, narrow streets and parked at a hotel. I checked my phone's navigation screen one last time and let out a victorious whoop. I'd been on the road for ten hours! I'd been an hour quicker than Google had estimated, too, despite twice spending some time lying down on the asphalt. I opened the curtain in my room and looked outside. Dusk cast dark shadows over the fields of tea that covered the mountains surrounding Darjeeling. I smiled. After so much time in the suffocating, disgusting air of Delhi, this was a breath of fresh air.

–

That night, my phone beeped to announce that my detailed travel itinerary from Osuga Myanmar Travels had arrived. I would have to hurry—I was expected in Moreh, the small Indian village by the border with Myanmar, in less than a week. I wasn't looking forward to riding with a group and following a set schedule, but I didn't have much choice—this was the only way to travel through the country. After a short ride through Sikkim the following day, I picked up speed and rode more than 600 miles through the northeastern states of India in a week.

–

Getting on my bike in the morning became my favorite moment of each day. With all my belongings loaded on it, there was barely enough room for me. I was practically wedged in, my large backpack behind me, the fuel tank in front of me, and my head safely contained in my helmet. As soon as I felt my bag against my back and the cheek pads of my helmet against my face, I felt ready for a new day of not knowing what lay ahead. My motorcycle clothes and my luggage pressed up against me made me feel like a swaddled baby, and I don't doubt I looked a little bit like one too. But I didn't care how dumb I looked—it gave me a sense of security. And I knew I needed to feel safe now that I'd taken a path where every day was uncharted and nothing was for certain. Tired, but happy to have made it, I finally reached the Indian side of the border with Myanmar.

I slept poorly that night in Moreh. I was nervous about my first border crossing on my bike. Sure, I'd bought a Carnet de Passage from Mr. Dossa, but I had no idea whether any of the documents were actually in order. On top of that, it wasn't even my name on the papers, it was Irfan's. Whether I would be able to cross the border with these papers still remained to be seen. Wouldn't the customs officers think I'd stolen the motorcycle? The room I was staying in was one of the worst I'd ever seen, which didn't help either. The walls were covered in mold, the light in the bathroom was broken (though perhaps that was for the best), and the air inside was stale. I slept in my linen sleeping bag liner because the sheets looked—and smelled—unwashed. Taking in all of my surroundings, I swallowed. How I missed my own house. Squeezing my eyes shut, I imagined walking up the stairs to the bathroom and drawing a bath. Eventually, I drifted off into a fitful sleep, dreaming not of crossing the border, but of a murderous notary who forced me to sign the sale documents.

We assembled at the bridge that marked the border between India and Myanmar at 8 a.m. the next morning. I was the only solo traveler; everyone else traveled in pairs. We made for a fascinating group, with a wide variety of motorcycles. Mikael and Kevin were Swedish and both rode small, light bikes: a Honda Grom and a CRF250L. An Austrian couple, Claudia and Peter, rode the largest and most heavily loaded motorcycle of the group: a Suzuki V-Strom 1000. Then there were Isaac and Chema, two Spaniards who each had a BMW GS. They had originally left Spain together but had fallen out on the road and continued separately. Ironically, neither had known the other would be on this trip, and neither seemed particularly enthused about their reunion when they saw each other that morning.

Last but not least was a Russian couple, Battal and Masha, who had traveled halfway across the globe on a completely unsuitable Honda VFR. They had more mechanical issues than anyone else and hadn't even made it to the border on time for our crossing. Our guide, Mying Kyaw, instructed us to go ahead so we could wait for them in Myanmar.

It wasn't long before I begrudgingly admitted to myself that I really didn't mind riding in a group. The Swedish Hondas confidently approached the border, followed by the Austrian couple. They had already crossed dozens of borders on their motorcycles, while I had no idea how any of this worked or what to do with the registration documents, customs formalities, or the yellow Carnet de Passage booklet. Now that I was with an experienced group, I could feel myself relax. Maybe this wouldn't be all that bad. To my great relief, not a single official asked who Irfan was or why the motorcycle wasn't in my name, and so I collected my first stamp in the yellow booklet. I tenderly held the Carnet de Passage to my chest for a moment. I'd made it—I had arrived in another country with my motorcycle!

Mr. Kyaw had the unenviable task of keeping the group together while keeping up the pace. We rode through the countryside of Myanmar for a couple of hours and stopped at a restaurant for lunch. We talked more than we ate, but I couldn't tell whether that was because of the unappetizing dishes or the excellent conversation. We all feverishly exchanged information about where we had been and where we were going.

Everyone at the table had done tens of thousands of miles through multiple countries. Just like that first night of my adventure on a rental bike with the Brits, I felt like a complete beginner. Battal pointed at the camera attached to my helmet.

"You film?" he asked. I nodded.

"Have you seen the *Long Way Round*?" asked Peter.

"No, what is that?" I asked. A brief silence fell while everyone at the table looked at me. Apparently, it was *the* must-see TV show for any aspiring motorcycle adventurer. But surely, I must have read *Jupiter's Travels* by Ted Simon, pioneer of motorcycle travel? I shook my head again.

"I'm only going from here to Malaysia, you know, it's not that far. My journey isn't as long as yours," I said defensively, lowering my eyes to the plate of food that sat on the table in front of me.

The following days we continued riding southeast through hilly terrain. We passed endless fields with a great variety of crops: green strips bursting with rice plants and corn, and a lot of sugar cane and tobacco as well. It was exhilarating to be back in Myanmar, my favorite country in Southeast Asia. I had many incredible memories of my previous visit, seven years before.

My warm sentiment for this country was a bit peculiar, though, because it's also where I had gotten seriously ill. I had contracted what would later turn out to be malaria in a remote, northern mountain village in Shan State. I was traveling alone, and because internet was only accessible from internet cafés in large cities back then, nobody knew exactly where I was. Delirious and with a sky-high fever, I realized with blinding clarity that if I died there, nobody in the village would know who I was—or care, for that matter.

I spent two days lying on a mattress in a hut, deathly ill and alone, but hunger and thirst eventually drove me outside. I forced myself to get on a bus and take the twelve-hour-long bumpy bus journey to the city of Mandalay, in search of a hospital. With my cheeks flushed bright red with fever, pain everywhere, and constantly throwing up out of the bus window from a fierce headache, I managed to drag myself to a hospital. They admitted me straightaway. My condition rapidly improved after a fairly aggressive course of treatment, but a deep-seated fear of malaria never left me.

Despite that unfortunate chapter, I had absolutely loved Myanmar. Tourism was almost nonexistent at the time, and the locals were incredibly friendly and polite. Compared to the busy beaches of Thailand and the hordes of scantily dressed young (and old) Europeans who roamed the streets there, Myanmar felt like the Asia I had always imagined. Both men and women wore beautiful floor-length *longyis*, made of colorful fabric that are wrapped around the waist. The women wore them as skirts and the men as skirtlike pants. Both genders also wore yellow makeup called thanaka, which they used to draw intricate patterns on their skin. The thanaka was decorative but also served as protection against the bright sun. There had been so much to see: from floating villages to pagodas adorned with tons of gold, centuries-old temple valleys and colorful markets.

They didn't have ATMs back then, so I had brought one thousand American dollars in cash, which I traded on the black market for piles and piles of Myanmar kyat. The kyat was worth so little that I spent weeks lugging a huge bag of cash around. I visited as much of the country as I could, which unfortunately didn't include the states around the border such as Mon, Kachin, Chin, and part of Shan State. The Myanmar government had designated these states as "unstable" due to clan fights and Thai rebels, so I was only allowed to visit the central parts of the country where the majority of the population was of the Bamar ethnicity.

Not much had changed on that front in the past seven years, and the ethnic conflict seemed to have intensified even further. Travel restrictions were tighter than they had been, and I was glad that I'd already seen so much of Myanmar on my previous visit. Because of that, I didn't mind as much the fact that I now had to power through the country in six days. It turned out that staying with the guide and government official's car wasn't enforced at all, and we had a lot more freedom than I had expected. Every day, Mr. Kyaw told us where we had to go that day, where our hotel was and what roads we were supposed to take, but we were free to ride there in our own time. I usually spent my days riding with the Austrians, Peter and Claudia. In the evenings everyone reconvened to continue our conversation about motorcycles and travels.

On the eve of our last day, Mr. Kyaw assembled the group. I could tell by the creased expression on his face that he had some news. "Tomorrow, cross border into Thailand," he said matter-of-factly. "Thailand, you need a guide too. But, we go to small border crossing, I hope not necessary there." A brief wave of murmurs rippled through the group, and a few people whooped.

"You're a hero, Mying," the Spaniard Chema said, speaking all our minds.

Thailand's new rule that you weren't allowed to ride a motorcycle through the country independently, but instead had to hire a Thai guide to travel with you, didn't make sense to any of us. Every half-baked tourist tore through the streets on rented mopeds, but we were supposedly not allowed to ride around freely on our own motorcycles? I hoped fiercely that I'd be allowed to make my own way again in Thailand, and not be stuck following another guide.

The ride to the border took a good three hours, and this time everyone kept together. I briefly felt like I was part of my own motorcycle gang and positioned myself at the center of the group. This would be my second time crossing a border on my motorcycle, and I already felt a bit more confident about the procedures than I had the first time. We passed through a decorated gate with the words "Republic of the Union of Myanmar" written on it in gold letters and parked our motorcycles in a neat single-file line. I collected my second stamp in my Carnet de Passage, and in the blink of an eye I'd been stamped out of Myanmar. Entering Thailand turned out to be a matter of various formalities and bureaucratic hoops to jump through. While filling out my umpteenth form, I briefly hovered my pen over the field labeled "profession." I glanced around and finally wrote "geologist." I wasn't too keen on officially fessing up that I didn't have a job at all.

A customs officer holding a stack of documents walked up to me and asked: "Chassis number?"

He had a round head with full, chubby cheeks that almost tempted me to give them a little squeeze. Instead, I focused on my motorbike. I honestly hadn't expected them to check the chassis number, but that was exactly what he came to do. I didn't have the faintest idea where to even find it, but luckily he was already bending over and pointing at the number stenciled in the frame, between the front forks.

"Ah, there it is," I said, pointing at the number too.

Then he looked at the engine number, and when that checked out as well, he disappeared back into the chaos that apparently always reigned at a border crossing.

I stood next to Basanti, feeling a bit lost. I knew I wanted to go to Chiang Rai from here, but other than that I had no plan. The prospect of continuing on my own didn't exactly shine on the horizon like some glorious beacon. Claudia caught my eye and smiled. As if she'd read my mind, she asked: "We're going to Chiang Rai next, want to ride with us?"

I nodded so emphatically that it made me laugh. When I looked at her again, she laughed too.

"Alright," said Claudia, "wait for us once you're through customs and we'll ride together."

We did, and after Chiang Rai we also rode to Chiang Mai together, but that's where we went our separate ways. Claudia and Peter wanted to stick around in Chiang Mai, but I was itching to keep going.

They saw me off at our hotel, and I quickly shut my visor as I felt my eyes welling up. A wave of affection suddenly washed over me. These two kind, modest Austrians had been my first real motorcycling friends. They had gotten me through my first border crossings and inspired me with their stories about journeying from Europe to India. I didn't know at the time that, thankfully, this would not be the last time we'd meet.

–

I had been looking forward to being alone again, but now that I was, I found it more difficult than I'd expected. I had always thrived on being alone. Some people jump from one relationship to the next, just to avoid being on their own—I wasn't like that, that much was certain. But solitude felt different since my painful breakup. I wished I'd never read those texts. I had gone through every sentence of them, uncovering every lie with the same diligence with which I'd written my master's thesis.

All at once I found myself taken back to that moment; how I'd stood in my bedroom, with my laptop in my hands. I could still remember what I was wearing, what sheets were on the bed, and how sick I had suddenly felt. In the months before, I had asked him point-blank if he was cheating on me multiple times, but he had always categorically denied it. He acted like I was crazy, and the longer that went on, the more I started to believe him. I didn't recognize the mistrustful, paranoid person I had become and hated that version of myself.

Eventually, I went looking for the answers I wasn't getting from him. I broke into his computer, where I found a Word document containing their complete WhatsApp conversation history. Dozens and dozens of pages, recording eighteen months of conversation between the two of them. I read every message they had exchanged and unraveled everything, lie by lie, down to the most intimate details. They had called me "N."

"Does N suspect anything?" she would ask him.

At the time, bringing the truth to light seemed so important to me that I read the document to the point of exhaustion. It's not surprising that certain sentences would still pop into my head months later, prompted or not. I recorded my motorcycle journeys, sent happy pictures to friends. As far as the outside world was concerned, I was living the dream, having the time of my life. But that wasn't my experience at all. If I'd had a magic wand that could rewind everything and turn my deceitful relationship into a loving one, I would have used it.

–

Forcing my sadness back into its cage, I turned the corner outside the hotel and looked ahead. I tried to keep my eyes focused on the road and my thoughts on Thai cuisine. Oh, the food in Thailand. With Myanmar's less appetizing offerings still fresh in my memory, I ate like I'd been starving for weeks. In reality it had just been six days, but it was true that I had barely eaten in Myanmar. The Myanmar cuisine is—how do I put this politely?—an acquired taste. Rice with pieces of raw chicken liver and chicken feet, pork intestines on a stick, eggs with half-developed duck embryos, and don't even get me started on the deep-fried mud balls made of tamarind. Even the vegetables were prepared in such a way that I just couldn't swallow them.

As I made steady progress from northern to southern Thailand, I started developing a steady routine. Every morning, I loaded all my worldly possessions onto my motorcycle, and every late afternoon I took it all off again. I dragged the whole shebang up flights of stairs to doors of hotel rooms and back down those same stairs the next day. My trip had evidently turned into an endless cycle of packing, unpacking, and hauling my bags back and forth in between. My biceps were starting to get disproportionately large from dragging my heavy backpack everywhere. I decided it was time for a small reorganization.

I'd taken notes on how Peter and Claudia had managed to transport two people's luggage on a single motorbike, and purchasing a top box like theirs seemed like a good place to start. I spent a few days in Bangkok, Thailand's capital, scouring motorcycle shops. Soon enough I was smugly taking in my Basanti 2.0.

Her new aluminum top case was lockable. It gave me a ton of extra storage space, and a waterproof duffel bag replaced the backpack I had been tying onto her back up to that point. I also bought a lightweight mesh motorcycle jacket, which would be a lot more comfortable in the tropical temperatures of southern Thailand. On top of that, I bought a hydration backpack. Now I was able to slip the hose of the reservoir under my helmet while riding so I wouldn't have to keep stopping whenever I wanted to take a sip of water. Lastly, I'd bought a Garmin navigation system so I wouldn't have to use my phone on my bike when it rained.

My new jacket turned out to be a good investment—it was a lot lighter and cooler than the bulky motorcycle jacket I'd been wearing so far. But the heat and humidity of southern Thailand still hit me like a pile of bricks, breezy jacket or not. I could cope with the heat as long as I was moving, but I dreaded every traffic light, every crossroad.

Basanti wasn't a huge fan of the warm climate either; her air-cooled engine became blistering hot. I may as well have pre-heated an oven to 400 degrees and placed it between my legs. In southern Thailand, I didn't sweat like a person any longer, but more like a block of cheese: sticky, moist, and emitting a cloying smell.

It came down in buckets a few times a day, but it never got any cooler. Sopping wet from the rain and my own sweat, I eventually reached my final overnight stop in Thailand, just under an hour's ride from the Malaysian border.

I crawled into the bed that felt more like a pile of clammy rags. Even when I lay completely motionless, not moving a muscle, rivulets of sweat ran down my body.

The following morning I rode away from the wooden cabin where I'd spent the night. I stopped at a small reception building to give my key to the cleaning lady, standing outside in her red apron.

"*Kap khun ka,*" I said. Thank you.

It wasn't long before I'd reached the Thai side of the border and found myself looking at a sign saying BON VOYAGE in bold letters. I wondered why they'd chosen the French wording, but when I discovered that the Thai translation was *kr hâi dern taang doi sà-wàt-dì-pâap*, it started to dawn on me. Border control on both sides was a well-oiled machine, and Basanti and I were stamped out of Thailand and into Malaysia without any issue.

I'd loved the food in Thailand, but in Malaysia I pulled out all the stops; the cuisine there was even *more* varied. Most menus had Chinese, Malay, Indian, and even Arabic influences. Local dishes were flavored primarily with lemongrass, galangal, kaffir lime leaves. I polished off entire plates of *nasi lemak* (coconut rice), filled up on *roti canai* (a kind of flatbread), and often even found *rendang* on the menu, which I knew to be an Indonesian dish. That was the plus side of losing all those grief pounds: I was in the perfect place to gain them all back again.

At breakfast, I invariably ordered a mug of strong coffee with condensed milk and so-called egg-toast. The toast was served on a plate and a semi-raw egg in a mug on the side. You then had to dump that over the toast yourself. It looked extraordinarily unappetizing but I couldn't get enough of it, it was that delicious.

Kuala Lumpur was quickly coming into view, and the air grew hotter and more humid the closer I got. I opened my helmet's visor as I rode and didn't even feel a teeny breeze. I'd departed from the Cameron Highlands that morning, a plateau almost five thousand feet above sea level, and it had been blissfully cool. There wasn't much left of that coolness now, and I had another 60 sweaty miles to go. After a good while of riding through the vast tea plantations of the highlands, I approached a small town. My navigation system told me to turn right, but when I did, I almost came down. It felt like my rear tire had lost all grip, and I awkwardly swerved through the bend.

"Oh, this isn't good," I said out loud. "Something's wrong."

I turned onto a side street, parked Basanti next to the curb, and dismounted to inspect my tires. Completely dumbfounded, I stared at my rear tire. There was no doubt about it: the tire was flat. In Karol Bagh, back in Delhi, they had injected some kind of black slime between my tire and the tube. The black goo was now bubbling out and running down one of my spokes.

"With this stuff, you'll never get a flat tire," Satnam had assured me. I had the unsettling hunch that he had been wrong. I shook my head in disbelief.

"But I was so close," I mumbled quietly.

As I was still coming to terms with the fact that my tire was really flat, I hadn't noticed a man and a woman approaching me from behind.

"You have a problem?" I heard suddenly.

I spun around. "Yes, I have a flat tire," I replied.

I was met with the friendly faces of a man wearing a colorful shirt and a young woman holding a black umbrella, even though it wasn't raining.

"Don't worry, I'll call a mechanic," the man said.

I sighed in relief. In Delhi, during my crash course in motorcycle mechanics, I had learned that when push came to shove, I couldn't fix a tire on my own. I didn't know where these people had come from, but I was glad for their unsolicited help. It wasn't long before the promised mechanic showed up. Without hesitating, he got to work and an hour after discovering my puncture, I had a new tube and was ready to carry on. I paid the mechanic double what he charged me and thanked everyone again. I realized that Southeast Asia might be the best place in the world to get a flat tire on your bike, seeing as how it had more mopeds and motorcycles than cars. Patching punctures was the most natural thing in the world here. I'd been lucky.

I finally reached modern, lively Kuala Lumpur after a long day of riding. It felt a bit surreal to navigate Basanti through its streets. What had sounded like a ridiculous plan back in Delhi didn't seem quite so crazy anymore. Apparently, I *could* just ride my motorcycle from India to Malaysia.

And yet, though I'd completed the itinerary I'd laid out for myself two months earlier, I didn't feel like I'd reached my final destination. In fact, it felt like I was just getting started. From the moment I'd entered Malaysia, I had started plotting my next adventure. I still had ten months before my Carnet de Passage expired and I'd have to return my bike to India. It would be a waste not to make use of that time.

I had also reached another milestone: one thousand subscribers on my YouTube channel, with a total watch time of four thousand hours. That meant I was eligible to become a YouTube partner and could start putting ads before and during my videos. Since leaving Delhi, I had recorded and edited thirty-seven episodes. I was tireless in my work rhythm—ride and film, edit; ride and film, edit. Although the views on my channel were far too low to earn me enough even to fill up Basanti's tank, it was still bigger than anything I'd achieved in months of blog writing. I felt like now was the time to push through.

–

I settled into my hotel room and spread my world map out on the bed. Standing there, bent over the map and tracing imaginary routes with my finger, I once again felt like the world was at my feet. The realization that I could do whatever I wanted sank in on a more profound level than ever before. I could go anywhere. I had the freedom to go, to stay, to say yes and—above all—to say no. My eyes were drawn to the Middle East, then to Central Asia, and suddenly, I knew. If I had my bike shipped to Oman, I could cross Central Asia from there, and then ride back to India via Tajikistan, Kyrgyzstan, and a bit of China. In doubling the length of my motorcycling adventure with a single decision, right there in that damp hotel room, I felt freer than ever.

Chapter 4

Spread Your Wings and Fly

Miles: 6,835

Global Airfreight. That was the name of the transportation company I had entrusted with the important task of bringing Basanti to Oman. My point of contact was a man named Anikolz, with whom I had rapidly exchanged dozens of emails before he invited me to a small, sketchy industrial park outside Kuala Lumpur to have a shipping crate built. From what he had told me, I would be paying either for the combined weight of the crate and its contents or simply for the crate's dimensions. It would therefore be cheaper if we managed to build the crate as small as possible. And so I'd already removed the fairings and rode to the agreed-upon address.

The building that supposedly housed the freight agency had big black stains on its facade. *Was that mold?* Pallets of blue barrels stood out front, looking like they were about to be shipped to a chemical plant. I hesitated briefly, but eventually parked and hopped off the bike.

A heavyset man wearing a black T-shirt that said "Gucci" in gold letters started down the stairs just when I was about to step inside. He had a thin mustache and a tuft of hair on his chin for a goatee. If you'd told me he was the undercover bodyguard of an Asian emperor, I would have believed you.

"You're here for Anikolz?" he asked.

"Yes," I said, relieved. "Did he tell you I would be here?"

"Yes, yes."

I took that as a sign that we would start building the crate. First I took off the side panniers, then the top box. There was still some gas in my extra fuel jerrycans, so I poured it into a plastic container and gave it to my new bodyguard. He was absolutely thrilled.

I was consumed by my mission to make the bike as compact as possible. So much so that I didn't realize that the other employees present at the industrial park who had been milling about had gone off to do something else. I was left alone with the pallets of blue, potentially poison-filled barrels and a semi-dismantled motorcycle. Unintentionally, I took on the role of watchman and sat down in a chair in front of the building to make sure nothing got stolen. Thankfully, one of the employees came back a little while later.

"I'm going to buy wood," he announced.

"For the crate?" I asked. A pretty silly question in hindsight, but I hadn't expected them not to already have it. I had assumed that this transportation company had shipped motorcycles before, but I turned out to have been given the questionable honor of being their very first. And so we didn't just go out to shop for wood, but also for nails. And a saw. And perhaps think up a plan for what to do with all of the above.

As we walked to the truck to set off, he told me: "First, we eat." Malaysia truly is a country after my own heart. He opened the passenger door of his truck for me and an empty soda can immediately tumbled out.

"Wow," he said.

It was as if he knew what I was thinking—wow. The cabin looked like a raccoon had been wreaking havoc in it for a good few weeks, although I was pretty sure Malaysia doesn't actually have any raccoons.

One plate of rice with chicken in delicious sauce later, he drove the truck to a lot with a large sign that read KAYU LAMA in red painted letters. "Old wood," was clearly what that meant. Unfortunately they were out of plywood. We left the second place we tried empty-handed as well. The third time was the charm, and we could finally start building our crate. Or rather, they could start building the crate while I watched and felt useless.

They nailed four wooden pallets together to make the base. It soon turned out that we needed more narrow pieces of wood, and operations had to be ceased because the stores had already closed their doors. It was the day before Chinese New Year, and everyone here had the next few days off. With Malaysia's sizeable Chinese community, I'd read that giving everyone the day off strengthened social ties and harmony between the various ethnic groups in the country. Everywhere in Kuala

Lumpur the streets and buildings were decorated with red lanterns, the symbolic color of luck and prosperity.

I made the most of this time. During the three days that followed, I could be found on Petaling Street, also known as Chinatown. I tasted the various market stalls' wares and was entertained by the colorful lion and dragon dances. The dancers were accompanied by rhythmic, traditional music played on drums, and they performed impressive choreographies. It was executed so exquisitely that I felt like I was in China.

–

Three days later, I got back into the truck and we went out once again to buy wood.

"So, how are you today?" I asked.

"Good. Thanks to Noraly, I come to work today," he said with a laugh. I awkwardly smiled back. I felt ashamed that I had spent so much time with this man without bothering to ask his name. Now it felt too late to do so, so I just looked out the window and kept my mouth shut.

We went to yet another store, and I bought more wood, nails, a tape measure and some superglue. While the others carried on with the pallets, I used a screwdriver to loosen the handlebar risers so I could move down the handlebars and lessen the height of the bike. I should have bought that tape measure before buying the plywood three days before, because of course everything *almost* fit—but not quite. Basanti was a couple of inches too tall for the sides we wanted to make with the plywood. This was exactly the kind of situation that would normally stress me out, but the relaxed attitude of the men I was working with had a calming effect. With the handlebars half unscrewed and pushed down, everything wound up fitting just right. Then I removed the battery and taped up the connections. According to Anikolz the customs officials would have taken care of that for me, but I couldn't imagine they made a habit of tinkering with the motorcycles they came across. And I didn't want to run the risk of encountering shipping problems because of something stupid, like a battery.

The crate was finished and I was invited along to the airport, so I could fill out the necessary paperwork and take care of customs formalities there. With the crate safely in the truck, I got in. There was another driver, and this time I did ask and remember his name: Faisal.

I thought I would be able to sort out the customs formalities within a day, but that turned out to be a tad optimistic. After dropping off the crate at the airport, I had to wait another four days before my Carnet de Passage had all the required stamps as well. Then everything started happening all at once. Anikolz called to tell me that Basanti would be loaded onto a cargo plane that same day. I hastily booked a flight for myself to Muscat, Oman's capital, for the next morning.

–

I stepped outside through the large sliding doors of Muscat airport and was hit by a wall of heat that almost blew me back into the terminal. The temperature was on par with what I'd experienced in southern Thailand and Malaysia, but this was a dry heat. Like a gigantic, hot hair dryer, the katabatic wind, or "Gharbi," blew dry air from the mountainous desert to the coastal areas, where Muscat was located. I stopped for a moment, inhaling deeply. Since leaving India, I'd only crossed land borders, and the temperature differences and smells had slowly blended into one another. I had missed the sharp contrasts that came after a long flight. My lips stretched into a grin. Oman smelled wonderful.

"Taxi, madam?" sounded a modest voice. I caught a taxi driver's eye and nodded. Mohammed skillfully took my bags and swung them into the trunk of his taxi. I slumped down onto the back seat and took out my phone to find my hotel reservation.

"To the A'Sinamar Hotel, please."

On our way to the hotel, I looked out the car window and thought about Basanti. *Dang it*, I thought, *I miss her already*. Even though it had been a piece of cake finding a taxi, I once again missed the independence my motorcycle gave me.

When I logged onto the hotel Wi-Fi, I saw from the tracking number I'd been given that the plane Basanti should have arrived on had never left Kuala Lumpur—and worse, it was delayed by two weeks. Two weeks! I flopped onto the bed feeling a bit lost. Two weeks felt like an insurmountable amount of time. What was I supposed to do with myself without my motorbike?

Nonetheless, it took me surprisingly little time to get Basanti out of my head and start researching bike rentals in Oman. Before long, I'd found Peter Middleton's website. With his company, Oryx Adventures, he organized off-roading tours and lessons. I chuckled quietly. A little late perhaps, but it wouldn't be a bad idea to finally get some off-roading instruction. It hadn't been long since I'd bounced down the Rohtang Pass in India. And with my new plan to ride through Central Asia, I knew there would be plenty more unpaved roads ahead of me. It was high time I properly learned how to ride a motorcycle.

–

Peter had a spot for me a few days later and I took a taxi to his house in Muscat. A Brit with a full head of curly brown hair, Peter had worked in the oil and gas industry for more than twenty years. That's how he had ended up in the Middle East, and in Oman. When he saw the country's incredible terrain but couldn't find a single company that organized motorcycling tours, he decided to start Oryx Adventures.

He didn't waste any time, immediately showing me the bike I'd be riding: a CCM with a 450cc BMW engine. I had never actually heard of that make before, but with twice the power and only half the weight of Basanti, I had a hunch that this was going to be fun. For three days, I rode with Peter as he taught me the basics of off-roading. How the bike felt when you braked hard in the sand, how to get through unpaved hairpin bends, how to maintain control on a steep descent, and how to ford rivers. These lessons were so important that they stuck with me like mantras. I still put them into practice years later.

In between lessons, I soaked up the spectacular beauty of Oman. There were rugged, stark mountains that surrounded green oases full of palm trees and turquoise waters. We rode through the Hajar mountain range that stretched across the northwest of the country and, with the motorcycles, climbed the Jebel Shams, the highest point of the Hajar mountains. I never knew that Oman was so inhospitably rugged and at the same time so rich in fertile valleys. I was glad to be riding with Peter, who knew the area like the back of his hand. The *wadis* we crossed—a kind of dry riverbed—looked harmless but could be very dangerous after rain. Not that it rained much there, but even light rainfall rapidly transformed them into powerful torrents that engulfed everything in their path. They were deadly.

Eventually, Basanti arrived at the Muscat airport, but to my dismay, customs wouldn't release her. I turned out to be the very first person to attempt to import a motorcycle through the airport, and the option "motorcycle" didn't exist in their system. One of the officials showed me his computer screen; I could import horses of all colors—gray, black, white, brown. But a checkbox for "motorcycle" was nowhere to be found. The computer said no.

When I came back from the airport for the second time, again disappointed and empty-handed, I almost knocked into the hotel owner as I walked in. I had chatted with him a couple of times before, and he had immediately given me a free upgrade to a luxury suite when I told him that my bike had been delayed by two weeks. He was a beautiful man, and he always looked well-groomed and stylish. He wore *nizwas* (handmade) leather sandals and a *dishdasha* (a long, loose white garment) that reached down to his ankles. These were made of lightweight cotton, ideal for Oman's hot desert climate. His *dishdasha* was decorated with subtle embroidery around the collar.

"And?" he asked, smiling.

I shook my head and sighed. "No. The computer system can't import a motorcycle, even though I keep trying to explain that this is a temporary import, not a permanent one. I didn't get anywhere, and I'm not quite sure what else I can do."

He listened politely and then shook his head as if to say: *What a load of nonsense.* He whipped out his phone, dialed a number, and started speaking in rapid Arabic, occasionally looking over at me reassuringly. I waited politely, not expecting his phone call to be of any help.

That was until he hung up his phone and said to me in English: "I own the airport."

Of course. "Ah," I managed to say.

His phone call put things quickly into motion, and an hour later my phone rang, the name "Faisal Customs" appearing on its screen. Faisal passed on that they still required a bunch of information from me, like the color of my bike, its make, a copy of Irfan's passport, and, above all, an answer to the question of who Irfan was.

A few hours later, when I was finally reunited with the wooden crate that had been painstakingly put together, my heart did a somersault. The top of the crate was pried open, and I quickly peered inside.

"She looks healthy," joked Faisal.

I could only agree with him. Once I had reconnected the battery and she started on the first attempt, I knew she was as fit as she looked.

A dozen airport employees waved me goodbye as I rode off with the biggest grin that would fit on my face. I'd done it. I'd actually done it.

Unfortunately, my euphoria didn't last long. As soon as I turned into the first corner, I felt that same weird wobble in my rear wheel as I had when I got a flat tire in Malaysia. But how was that possible? I had fully serviced Basanti in Kuala Lumpur and replaced the worn-down tires as well as the tubes. In fact, I had gone even further and had the bike pretty much completely stripped. I wanted to be sure that it would be in perfect condition for the next part of my journey. The tear in the swingarm of that rental bike in Manali had sprouted, like a seed, into a deeply rooted distrust of Royal Enfield. I assumed I'd most likely lose all kinds of parts as my journey progressed, eventually blowing up the entire engine in a dramatic cloud of white smoke. That's why I had brought so many spares from Delhi: a complete clutch assembly, three oil filters, two air filters, a clutch cable, half a gallon of engine oil, brake pads, fuses, four tubes, a set of sprockets, and a chain. I had practically chopped up a motorcycle and stuffed half the pieces into my panniers. I'd seen plenty of Royal Enfield dealers in India—and to my surprise in Thailand and Malaysia as well—but I suspected these didn't exist in Central Asia. I wanted to avoid having to spend weeks waiting for parts to arrive in Uzbekistan or Tajikistan.

Luckily, my head had gone into a tailspin over nothing. When I stopped to check the pressure in my tires, they turned out just to be a bit soft after having been tied up so tightly for the flight. I regained a bit of faith in my beloved Royal Enfield.

–

I spent the following week exploring the east coast of Oman, visiting Masirah Island and riding north straight through the desert, toward the land border with the United Arab Emirates. It immediately gave me a chance to put Peter's lessons into practice on a fully loaded motorcycle.

Although I was a long way from participating in the Dakar Rally, I could finally hold my own a little better on tricky off-road sections.

I had never crossed a desert on my own before, let alone on a motorcycle, but I loved it instantly. The vast, open landscapes practically begged to be traversed. Time and time again, it gave me a sense of perfect autonomy. I could steer Basanti across any random narrow path through the desert—wherever I wanted to go. I solemnly swore to myself to never again ride a city bike like my old Ducati and limit myself to paved roads.

Oman was the first country I'd visited that was a sultanate. As far as I knew, Brunei was the only other country in the world with this form of government. Oman's Sultan Qaboos bin Said al-Said had been in power there since 1970, only to pass away at the age of seventy-nine less than a year after my visit. The country had gone through major changes under his leadership. In fifty years' time, Oman had modernized and built schools, hospitals, and roads. I had noticed how even the smallest, most remote villages were connected to the electricity network. The Omanis I asked about this told me that Sultan Qaboos had built the infrastructure for them. He had also played a crucial role in encouraging religious tolerance. Freedom of religion was guaranteed by the constitution of Oman, and although the country was primarily Muslim, non-Muslims had the right to practice their own religion. This also meant I didn't have to wear a hijab. Everywhere I went I felt welcomed by the Omanis, treated with respect, politeness, and warmth.

Despite their generous hospitality and the country's stunning natural beauty, I couldn't stick around for long. I had just received my visa for Iran, which I had applied for while I was still in Kuala Lumpur. I was itching to leave the Arabic peninsula and cross to Iran by boat.

There was a part of me that wanted to live more in the moment and travel more slowly. This better version of myself would take her time riding around, unhurriedly stopping to take photos, not leaving a country until she was sure she had seen everything. But that's just not me. My hunger for that which lies behind the next curve, behind the next mountain range, and in the next country, was simply too great.

To justify it to myself, I often said: "Always leave something undiscovered for next time. Then you'll have a reason to come back." To me, this seemed like an excellent excuse for my restlessness. If I repeated it to myself enough times, I would start to believe it eventually. Right?

I reached the border between Oman and the United Arab Emirates without any issue. The ferry to Iran didn't depart from Oman itself, but from the emirate of Sharjah. To get to Iran, I would first have to enter the United Arab Emirates. At Oman's border office, it didn't take long for a group of curious bystanders to gather around me. Most of them wore a *dishdasha*, and some a *kumma*—a cylindrical, embroidered hat with a flat top that was part of Oman's traditional dress. Others had tied colored turbans around their head, and I wondered if they were perhaps Emiratis from Dubai or one of the six other emirates. The customs official who stamped my Carnet de Passage was called Khalid and he had a short dark beard and jet-black, twinkling eyes. "Do you speak Arabic?" he asked with a smile. I liked him right away.

"Alhamdulillah," I answered uncertainly. *Praise be to God.* Khalid's coworker, who had joined the conversation, did not look impressed by this. "But Arabic is difficult," I protested.

"It's not difficult," he said. "You can easily learn."

"I only know *Alhamdulillah* and *shokran* (thank you)." He began to laugh. *"Wahed,"* I said, in an ultimate attempt to impress. I don't think I've ever tried to wow someone with the word for "one." I hesitantly continued, *"Ithnayn"* (two), *"hamsah"* (five). I realized that my attempt at counting to ten made no sense and gave up. My Arabic had been pretty decent a few years back, but just like with all the other languages I'd learned, I forgot them twice as fast when I didn't use them.

–

From the border, I followed the wide highway for an hour and a half until I arrived in the city center of Dubai. I rode through the deep gullies of buildings dozens of stories tall. This surreal, absurd, completely over-the-top cityscape did nothing for me. When snowy enclosures with live emperor penguins and ice rinks are being built in sandy deserts, we should probably ask ourselves what on earth we're all doing.

The neighboring emirate, Abu Dhabi, was of a similar order of insanity, but I had a good reason to ride there before taking the boat to Iran: to secure my visa application for Turkmenistan. I'd heard through the travelers' grapevine that Turkmenistan was a very difficult place to enter, and that the visa application process was long and convoluted.

The embassy in Abu Dhabi was known for approving a disproportionately high percentage of the visa applications they received. And if I applied in Abu Dhabi, my application could be processed while I traveled through Iran, reaching me just in time to enter Turkmenistan. At least, that was the idea.

I had been to Dubai a number of times for my job with the dredging company. But I'd also been to three other emirates: Fujairah, Sharjah, and Ras Al-Khaimah. I had never been to Abu Dhabi, Ajman, or Umm Al Quwain (apart from the Abu Dhabi airport, but that obviously didn't count). I looked forward to being able to check off emirate number five. I didn't quite see myself as an obsessed "country collector" whose sole goal was to be able to brag about having been to every country in the world. That wasn't very important to me, or even a compelling idea, truthfully. An ambition like that would mean visiting countries where horrible wars were raging or where diseases like Ebola were roaming free, or flying to all sorts of obscure islands in the middle of the Pacific. And yet I really wanted to see Abu Dhabi, if just to know what it was like.

On the morning of my appointment with the Turkmenistan embassy in Abu Dhabi, a thick, impenetrable fog sat atop the highway. I was freezing. It wasn't what I had expected of Abu Dhabi at all. By the time I'd filled out all the forms and handed an entire forest's worth of paperwork to the ambassador, the fog had thankfully lifted. I decided to ride a lap around Abu Dhabi and see some of the emirate. I rode past the gigantic Sheikh Zayed Grand Mosque Centre and marveled at its grandeur. Similarly to how Dubai wanted, seemingly more than anything, to have the tallest building in the world (resulting in the 2,700-foot-tall Burj Khalifa), Abu Dhabi had its own megalomaniac streak. Its Sheikh Zayed Grand Mosque Centre was one of the largest in the world, with space for more than forty thousand worshippers and boasting the world's largest hand-knotted rug (made in Iran) and the biggest chandelier in the world (from Germany). Outside, more than eighty marble domes gleamed in the sunlight, and inside it wasn't only marble shimmering but gold adornments, semiprecious stones, and crystals sent sparkles across the main prayer hall. I could only attest that this mosque was indeed a true spectacle.

The ferry to Bandar Abbas in Iran departed from Port Khalid, about a half hour's ride from Dubai in the emirate of Sharjah. Nerves jittered in my gut. I didn't know much about Iran, other than that it wasn't exactly known as a holiday destination. And what I had read or seen in the news was usually not very positive. But my curiosity about ancient Persia was greater than my doubts. The modern, futuristic extravagance of Dubai had only made my desire to go to Iran stronger. I wanted to see the beautiful architecture, the famous Persepolis, and the Persian gardens. And I wanted to experience the country of Persian poets like Rumi. After all, it had been Rumi who said: "Don't grieve. Anything you lose comes round in another form" and "You are not meant for crawling, so don't. You have wings. Learn to use them and fly."

The day before my departure, I swung by the Royal Enfield dealership and the Free Spirit motorcycling shop. Dubai had unexpectedly emerged as a social highlight of my journey, and I had made many new friends in the past week, whom I wanted to say goodbye to. They had treated Basanti to an oil change, a thorough clean, and an extensive checkup. I'd gotten a bunch of gifts from Sarah Kashyap, who worked for Royal Enfield, including a special pin that she stuck on my motorcycle jacket, and brand-new motorcycle gloves. That it would be these beautiful gloves that would endlessly torture my hands in the mountains of Tajikistan was something I was still blissfully unaware of.

PART 2

The pain, the risk, the fear, and the fight are as much part of the climb as the height itself.

Chapter 5

Not One of the Desert Folk

Miles: 8,450

I woke up under a wonderfully clean, white duvet in a large hotel room in Bandar Abbas. When I dug out my phone from under my pillow and saw the time, I jerked up—it was late. Quickly kicking off the duvet, I got out of the bed and, still groggy, teetered to the bathroom. The previous night on the ferry and the endless border procedures to get into Iran that followed had taken more out of me than I'd expected. I cupped my hands under the faucet and splashed cold water on my face. It helped a little.

I got dressed and spent a few minutes fidgeting with the thin scarf I'd used as a hijab for the first time the night before. I didn't quite manage to tie it in such a way that it stayed put. Every time, the whole thing would slide back and reveal blond locks of hair. Thinking I would be covering it up with my helmet soon anyway, I gave up and left it as it was. In a hurry, I dragged my bag to the hotel reception and checked out.

I wanted to ride about 250 miles that day to reach the town of Rayen. By this point in my travels, I knew I could easily cover that kind of distance if the roads were good. But I didn't know anything about the road conditions in Iran yet, so I assumed the worst—just to be on the safe side. I gave my hijab one last tug and then put on my helmet. From the corner of my eye, I saw the receptionist peeking sneakily at me from behind his desk and I pretended not to notice. I always felt uncomfortable when people watched me preparing to pull away, because those were exactly the moments I did something stupid, like stall the bike.

I started Basanti and rode off the hotel lot, past a row of tall, waving palm trees. I stopped at the first gas station I passed to fuel up.

"Russian?" asked the heavyset attendant, who towered over me like some kind of giant. He had so much long black hair on his lower arms that it knotted together in tight little curls.

"Holland," I said.

"Holland," he repeated, then shouted to his coworker that I was from the Netherlands.

"Robben, Robben," he added.

"Yeah, yeah, Robben." I laughed. Arjen Robben, the legendary Dutch soccer player. No matter how hard I tried to learn foreign languages, soccer eventually turned out to be the universal dialect.

When my tank was full, I fished out a stack of Iranian banknotes from my pocket. They had different denominations, with one worth one million rial. Their hyperinflation had gotten completely out of control. I had no clue how the amount on the pump compared to the money in my hands. This was because Iran had two currencies: the Iranian rial (IRR) and the Iranian toman. The toman was technically a subunit of the rial; one toman equaled ten rial. But I didn't understand how I was supposed to know if the pump showed the amount in toman or rial, and what notes belonged to which currency. The soccer-loving giant could have fed me any expensive lie he wanted to, but he didn't. I owed him 9,200 toman, and when I gave him a 10,000 bill, he gave me a 1,000 bill back. Instead of swindling me, he'd even given me a two hundred toman discount. This may not have been very much, but still. For a gallon of gas, I paid the equivalent of about three dollars.

–

The cheapest gas I'd found up to that point had been in Kuwait. A few years before, when I was sent there as a geologist, I paid less than a dollar per gallon. It was so ridiculously cheap there that gas station attendants would quickly spray gas over dusty windshields by way of service, to clean them. A gallon of gas was cheaper than a gallon of water, and apparently it wouldn't spontaneously combust your car. They didn't overthink things in Kuwait.

Truth be told, I had hated it there. I'd been sent in the dead of summer to look for sand. Part of me had found that hysterically funny:

a Dutch dredging company managing to sell sand to a country like Kuwait, which was essentially one big sandbox. But just like "the new gold" in Indonesia, they had a shortage of coarse building sand. The fine sand in the backyard of Kuwait City was unusable. And so I was sent out to sea with an offshore drilling rig and an Egyptian crew, since the right kind of sand *could* be found off the coast. It piled up on the hard seabed, sort of like underwater dunes. The men and I spent weeks drilling for sand in the blistering heat. If that weren't miserable enough, the men had the additional misfortune that Ramadan fell in summer that year, so they weren't allowed to take so much as a sip of water in the daytime. They spent entire grueling days putting together rods on the platform outside, the mercury hitting almost 120 degrees. It was a small miracle that nobody succumbed to the heat that summer.

One of the Egyptians did almost drown though, right before my eyes. It happened one morning, as we were trying to board the platform while a strong wind whipped the ocean into tall, wild waves. Every single day I waged another battle with this Egyptian man and his big, black mustache. He consistently refused to wear his life vest. He just wouldn't listen to me, even though I was his superior.

"I, strong swimmer," he would say.

His build made me doubt that. He was short and stocky, with a big, round belly. "I'm sure, but you're still wearing your life vest," I would insist.

Things went wrong that morning when he attempted to make the jump to the platform's ladder. Instead he fell short, and immediately went right under. Three of us managed to pull him out, coughing and heaving. That was also the last morning I ever had to mention the words "life vest."

–

I thanked the Iranian giant for the gas, said goodbye, and rode off with my tank full. Before I had even made it out of Bandar Abbas, I'd been cut off three times and nearly pushed off the road twice. I knew Iran had the highest number of traffic deaths in the world, but I had never understood why until now. Iranians drove like maniacs. They acted like they were driving getaway cars, zipping back and forth across the road to overtake each other. I didn't understand how there were any Iranians left who *weren't* hospitalized with a coma from an accident.

What they loved even more than speeding was watching me ride. They honked, waved, and took pictures of me from their moving cars. They got so excited that they would drive up next to me as closely as possible to spur me on. I was terrified that they might hit my side pannier and cause me to crash, but luckily that never happened. Thankfully, the more distance I put between myself and the city, the quieter the roads got. I finally started to relax.

I spent the rest of the day riding through the Zagros Mountains, the biggest mountain range in Iran. They stretch over 930 miles, from the border with northern Iraq to the southern part of the Persian Gulf. The collision between the Arabian and Eurasian plates had created these mountains, which had acted as the border of Mesopotamia in ancient times. On the other side of the mountain range lay the Iranian plateau, where crops such as barley and wheat had been domesticated for the first time in human history. This was where the town of Rayen, my destination for the day, was located, at an altitude of over 7,200 feet.

I passed through green, fertile valleys and crossed wide, sweeping rivers, riding past alternating tall and short mountains. My preconceived expectation of an Iran that mostly consisted of bone-dry deserts turned out to be completely wrong. I actually wasn't sure how I'd gotten that image in the first place. I steadily climbed to the top of the plateau, and the further I rode, the colder it got. I stopped by the side of the road to put my black motorcycle jacket on. It felt like a century since I'd last worn it. This was my original motorcycle jacket, the one I had brought from the Netherlands to India, and which had been far too warm for me in Thailand. I had considered getting rid of it to save space, but at that moment I was glad I still had it. Around dusk, I finally reached Rayen, stopping at the first building that looked like a hotel.

–

The next morning, still rubbing the sleep from my eyes, I took a good look around my hotel room. "Room" wasn't even the right word for it—I was in a huge apartment. There was a living room, a kitchen, and two bedrooms. Thanks to the hyperinflation in Iran, the apartment had cost me less than twenty dollars a night. I hauled my things down the stairs into the basement, where I'd parked my bike, and left Rayen. I had a strange feeling of excitement in my stomach. I always had this feeling when I went to a place I was intensely curious about, but which terrified me at the same time. It felt like the butterflies of a crush, but instead of fluttering cheerfully, their wings desperately beat against my stomach lining in an attempt to escape. I entered the Dasht-e Lut desert. Iran may not have been one big desert, but that wasn't to say that there were no deserts there at all. In fact, this desert was known as the hottest place on earth; a NASA satellite had once recorded a surface temperature of 159 degrees there. It was one of the most inhospitable places in the world. I wasn't sure exactly how far into the desert I would go, but it was said that the deeper into the Dasht-e Lut you went, the more beauty there was to see.

I followed the road toward the desert, and before long I had to stop to switch motorcycle jackets again. I was sweating so much as I rode that the T-shirt I wore under my jacket was soaked through. I put on my light mesh jacket and scrunched the black one under the bungee cords on the back of my bike. A few miles before the exit to the spectacular rock formations I planned on seeing, I saw a group of odd-looking trees on my left. They were set a bit back from the road, and with the mountains in the background, I was picturing an incredible photo. All I had to do was ride there and park Basanti in front of the trees. I quickly made a decision and left the asphalt. There was no path to the trees, but it looked flat enough to just ride there.

I'd barely gone three hundred feet when I realized I had made a serious miscalculation. I had ridden right onto a *sabkha*—a salt flat where the top looks like a hard crust, but which can be so thin that you can sink right through it. Though I didn't let up on the throttle, Basanti was noticeably slowing down, until eventually I came to a complete stop and felt both wheels sink into the salt flat. Panicking, I gave it full throttle and tried to engage the clutch. My rear wheel spun like a tornado, catapulting chunks of *sabkha* into the air, but I didn't move an inch. Soon enough, I felt so much heat coming off the engine that I was afraid I'd blow it up. I turned the key in the ignition and got off. *I have to give the engine a few minutes to cool down*, I thought. In the meantime, I scanned my surroundings. I spotted the main road I'd arrived on some distance behind me. The trees, which had looked so intriguing from there, now looked utterly mundane. This had been so stupid. I'd gotten myself into trouble, and for what? Just a pretty picture.

I grabbed the plastic hose from behind my shoulder and drank some water from my hydration pack. The water had gotten so warm that I might as well have been drinking flavorless tea.

After a few mouthfuls, I turned the key again and made another attempt at getting free. This time, I tried standing next to my bike so I could push on the handlebars and give throttle at the same time. It didn't work right away, but I kept trying until I began to smell something burning. I abruptly let go of the throttle and sniffed suspiciously at the air around me. Did I really smell that? Where was that smell coming from? Was it my rear tire, or maybe my clutch? I didn't know. I turned my head and looked at the road again. A sigh escaped me when I saw a car coming in my direction in the distance. I wildly kicked at the side stand, propped my bike onto it and ran, half-stumbling, toward the road. I waved both my arms in the air hoping they'd see me.

I have no idea what went through those three men's heads when they saw a helmeted figure running through the desert, but they stopped. Their doors swung open and they hurried toward me.

"Problem?" called the first one to reach me. He spoke English!

"Yes," I panted, half out of breath. Running three hundred feet across a salt flat in full motorcycle equipment, including a helmet, was no easy thing.

"I'm stuck. Really stuck. Can you push me?" He nodded and shouted something at the other two men, who were approaching as well. I climbed back onto the seat and the three of them pushed hard against my panniers. My rear wheel instantly began to move, gained some traction, and I lurched forward. I tried to turn, to point myself back in the direction of the asphalt as quickly as possible, but after just a few feet I sank back into the salty crust and the three men had to push me out again. This time I managed to ride all the way back to the road, where I stopped next to their car; they'd left it there, doors still wide open. I waited until they had reached me and got off my bike to properly thank them.

I kept repeating: "Thank you, thank you, really. Thank you." The three men laughed a little and shook their heads. They seemed just a bit younger than me. I wanted to ask them where they were coming from and where they were going, but before I could say anything they jumped back into their car, slammed the doors, and drove off. Two arms were stuck out of the windows to give me a final wave, and then they were out of sight.

My head was overheated from struggling with the bike and my heart was still racing. I cautiously took off in the same direction as the three men, resolving to stay on the paved road. That only worked for a few miles though, because I had already reached the exit leading to the Kaluts, a unique rock and sand dune formation that supposedly looked like eroded sandcastles.

Again, my inner geologist was determined to make a detour to see them with my own eyes, but the motorcyclist in me wasn't so sure. I hesitated. If there was more *sabkha* here, I might get stuck again. I didn't feel the need to relive that particular experience. I scanned the ground and spotted a tire track from a car. As long as I didn't run into any half-sunken cars, this track should be safe enough to follow. I accelerated, and a few minutes later I was surrounded by hundred-foot-tall Kaluts. I also found the car that had made the track. As I approached, an Iranian family stepped out. A young woman saw me and walked toward me. She was filming herself on her phone, which was blasting loud music. It was a remix of the song "Setareh" by the Iranian-Armenian singer Martik.

"Very good," she exclaimed in English. "Please, picture!" She pointed at her phone.

"Yeah, okay," I said.

She raised her arm holding the phone and counted as I struck a pose. "One, twoooo, three!" She beamed at me. "Thank you!"

She wore a cap over her hijab, just like her younger sister. Her brother had tied a checked scarf around his head, similar to how they wear them in Saudi Arabia. We chatted for a while and then went our separate ways again. I took a small lap around the Kaluts taking in the unbelievable formations. They were as magnificent as I'd hoped. I then stopped at a turnoff to an unpaved trail that would lead me deep into the Lut Desert. If I followed this trail, it would bring me to places with exciting names, such as the Rig-e Yalan dunes, the Snake Tongue Canyon, the Eye of the Lut (a mysterious salt lake), and a cluster of white star dunes that I believed to be unnamed. It was an unpaved desert route of about 87 miles on which I would be almost guaranteed not to meet any other people. This trail was what I'd been so excited and nervous about that morning. But standing there, my moronic incident on the salt flat still fresh in my memory, I chickened out. I had already tested my luck once today, and I just couldn't assume it would stick with me for another incident.

Sometimes I wish I had a fraction of the confidence that my good friend Mireille has. She is the most optimistic and self-assured woman I know.

"I have never tried that before, so I think I should definitely be able to do that," had supposedly been said once by Pippi Longstocking, but Mireille actually lived it. I wouldn't call myself a pessimist, but my confidence had gotten a dent the size of a frontal collision, and I could have used some of hers in that moment.

I felt as if I was being pulled in two different directions. The desert exuded a kind of magical attraction that very nearly forced me to ride on. But there was also a vague, ominous fear deep in my gut. Once again, after a moment of humiliation, I found myself unsure of which path forward to take.

I was from the Netherlands and hadn't been raised by desert folk. As a matter of fact, I knew very little about deserts, except that they could be lethal. Never underestimate the desert, someone had once told me. And this wasn't just any desert—this was the most scorchingly, blisteringly hot, hot, hot desert in the whole world. And ultimately that's what pulled me across the line, or rather: pulled me away from it. I turned around and got the hell out of there.

–

That night was Nowruz, Iranian New Year. It isn't celebrated on January 1, but at the start of spring, when day and night are equally long. There, the spring equinox marks the start of the new year and the awakening of nature. I found it quite a beautiful thought. The owner of the hotel I checked into that night had pointed it out to me.

"This night Nowruz," he said.

"Ah, tonight already?"

"Yes, one o'clock, people will start to clap. New year change."

"Oh really? At one o'clock," I asked, surprised. "Why not twelve o'clock?"

He didn't reply, but I later understood it had something to do with the astronomical calculations of scientists and calendar-makers of the spring equinox on a specific location. I told myself I'd stay up till 1 a.m. to see if there were any fireworks, but I was so exhausted that I was out like a light the second my head hit the pillow.

–

The next day, I had traveled just 93 miles toward the city of Yazd, located in the heart of the country on the Iranian plateau, when I was pulled over by the police. I parked Basanti by the side of the road and arranged my face into a relaxed, "everything under control, I obviously belong here" expression. As the police car came to a halt beside me, its window rolled down.

I opened my helmet's visor and peered inside the car. The shock wave that rolled through the officers was so intense that I could feel it. *A woman! It was a woman!*

"Are you alone?" one of the officers asked in English, staring at me in astonishment.

"Yes," I replied.

"Aren't you afraid, all alone on your motorcycle?"

"Sometimes," I replied vaguely. "But usually not."

I didn't know if he understood me, but he didn't say anything else. The window rolled back up and they drove off. Less than 3 miles later, the exact same thing happened, only with another police car. The officers were amazed at seeing a woman on a motorcycle, asked me whether I was alone, and then left. Not long after that, patrol car number three approached me. I suspected that their colleagues had already told them about me. From the corner of my eye, I could see in my mirror how the car turned and came after me. I went ahead and stopped so they wouldn't have to chase me down, lifting my helmet's visor yet again.

"Where are you going?" this officer asked when he and his partner stopped next to me. He wore a green military uniform and matching cap, making me wonder for a moment if he was army rather than police.

"To Yazd," I said.

He said something to his partner and the two of them smiled at me. "Alone?"

"Alone."

They spoke amongst themselves again and then he said: "It's dangerous, we're coming with you."

"That's really not necessary, really, I'm not scared," I protested.

"No, no," he said. "We're coming with you."

He said it with such a deep tone of authority that I didn't have much choice but to accept the escort. For 37 miles, they essentially tailgated me. I kept watching my mirror in the hope that they'd suddenly be gone, but they stayed right on my heels.

I had no idea why this was supposedly a dangerous area. We passed through an arid, open landscape with stunning mountains, on a neat but nearly deserted asphalt road. At first I was bummed because I couldn't stop to take pictures, then I was bummed because I really needed to pee. Usually, I would just pick a quiet moment to do my business in the bushes by the side of the road, but now I couldn't. With a full bladder, I wiggled from left to right on the seat of my motorcycle and tried to decipher from my navigation system when we'd pass through a village.

Out of nowhere, my escort suddenly overtook me and started driving very slowly, indicating that I needed to stop. They'll probably leave me alone now, I thought. I could almost feel the relief that would come when I emptied my bladder. Instead, I understood from the officers that they'd reached the end of their district, and that we would be waiting there for another escort from the next police district. We stood by the side of the road for a while, as I began hopping from one leg to the other faster and faster.

Eventually, they came to the conclusion that their colleagues weren't going to show up and that I would just have to carry on alone.

"No problem," I shouted, climbing back onto my motorcycle, my gloves only halfway on my hands. I took off with almost-screeching tires, my eyes already squinting to find a suitable bush or tree. None came, and instead there was consistently at least one car or truck in view. I entered the town of Bafgh and lo and behold, there was a small building with public bathrooms. I parked and with an odd waddle managed to reach it just in time.

I was just exiting the bathroom when I saw a TV crew waiting for me beside Basanti. I felt caught, as if my pants were still around my knees. I glanced down, just to be sure, but thankfully they weren't. I quickly fixed my hijab and walked toward the small group of people that had assembled. A man wearing a dark purple shirt and blue vest was waiting for me with a large microphone. A young woman wearing a black *chador* (kind of like a burqa, but where the face is left uncovered) was ready with the camera.

"How you from?" asked the journalist in broken English.

"From Holland," I replied.

"Please, welcome to Bafgh," he said.

"Thank you." I didn't know what else to say.

"Welcome to Bafgh and please go to the tourist," he said, pointing at the opposite side of the traffic circle.

"Tourist?" I couldn't make heads or tails of what he was saying.

"You. Go to tourist and television."

Eventually, I understood that he wanted me to come to the other side and that we would film there. Obligingly, I rode Basanti around the traffic circle and stopped at something resembling a market stall. There, the interview began. He asked me why I had come to Bafgh (to pee and have lunch, though I didn't bother to mention the first bit) and what kind of sights there were to see in Bafgh, Yadz, and Kerman (beautiful mosques). He had me shout "Welcome to Bafgh" at the camera a few times, and with that, the interview was over. I got a cup of tea and a fan with the words KHOSH AMADID printed on it, which meant "welcome." Despite the somewhat stilted interview, my interviewers had succeeded: I really did feel welcome in Bafgh, and in Iran.

–

After buying and devouring a lamb sandwich, I rode from Bafgh to Yazd, which seemed like a good location from which to explore the surrounding villages. I fell in love with Yazd from the moment I got there. The narrow alleyways, bustling bazaars, mud-brick houses, and streets teeming with traditional Iranian architecture; everything breathed history. It was one of the oldest inhabited cities in the world with a history that went back more than three thousand years. Delighted, I admired it all as I rode through the old town center toward a hostel. This was the Iran I'd longed for while I'd been staring at Dubai's modern skyscrapers. I had always felt more at home in places with a rich history than where everything was new. I'd hated Rotterdam as a city when I was a teenager, despite going to school there and it even being my place of birth. The bombings during World War II had completely obliterated the old city center. Although the new buildings were often viewed as architectural marvels, I had never liked them. On the other hand, I was immediately smitten with Utrecht when I went to college there. The first apartment I bought in Utrecht was the ground floor of an old house built in 1910.

The hostel I was staying in now had a lovely courtyard full of flowers and a characteristic *badgir*, a wind catcher. These towers gave Yazd its distinctive skyline, and I was fascinated by how this natural air-conditioning worked. The towers had multiple openings on top to catch wind. That air then traveled down through the tower toward the building, while being cooled along the way through contact with the tower's walls. The cool air was then led through various channels and vents into the interior of the building, driving out the warm air along the way. The people of Yazd had cooled their homes in this way for centuries, without the use of electricity.

I left my things at the hostel and took some excursions on Basanti without luggage. At an hour's ride to the northeast, I visited Kharanaq. This was a thousand-year-old ghost town, abandoned ages ago. During its prime, Kharanaq had been a stop on the Silk Road, where it had been a *caravanserai*: a resting place for the caravans of merchants and travelers who voyaged along the historic trading route. They could find shelter here, protection for themselves and their animals, and stock up on supplies. The entire village was built out of mud-brick, and the color of the houses was exactly like that of the surrounding landscape. Thanks to the village's camouflage, I imagined you could pass by it without even realizing. There were mosques, bathhouses, wind towers, and *qanats* (underground irrigation canals). When modern methods of transportation emerged, like railroads and motorized vehicles, the village was gradually abandoned until there was nobody left—except me.

I strolled through the eerily quiet village and wandered its alleyways for a while. One thousand years of history lay beneath my feet. Here and there some houses had collapsed, but I was surprised by how many of them were still proudly standing upright after all this time.

I left Kharanaq and rode straight through the Kavir desert to a place called Chak Chak in a dead-end ravine. To my surprise, it was packed when I arrived. I parked Basanti next to a car. In my full motorcycle gear with a scarf that kept trying to slip off my head, I ascended the 230 steps leading to the Fire Temple. The temple was dedicated to Anahita, one of the most important goddesses of Zoroastrianism.

I was ashamed to admit that I'd never even heard of Zoroastrianism before. I had undoubtedly learned about it in religious studies in high school, but I couldn't remember. It was an old religion, founded around 1500 B.C. in Iran, and had once been the predominant religion of the Persian Empire. Zoroastrianism preached the worship of one god, Ahura Mazda, but also recognized other divine beings that were personifications of divine qualities. The goddess Anahita, for example, was associated with fertility, water, and healing. The rise of Islam in the seventh century A.D. eventually caused a decline in Iran's Zoroastrian community, however. Yazd is one of the main areas where Zoroastrianism is still practiced, and that was also why Nowruz, one of the religion's oldest and most important holidays, was still a lively celebration here. I had unwittingly come to the Zoroastrians' most important pilgrimage point in its busiest week of the year. Now I understood why it was swarming with people.

When I reached the top step in front of the temple, I had to take off my shoes. My fellow visitors and I shuffled into the Fire Temple like sardines in a can, past a metal door with an image of a soldier holding a spear. Fire Temples were centers of worship, because fire was seen as a symbol of purity and divine light. I entered a small cave of sorts, with a wet marble floor and a gold chandelier hanging above a lotus-shaped fire tray. It smelled like incense and candles. A priest murmured prayers as he watched over the flames; Zoroastrians believed those flames should never be extinguished.

I heard a drop of water fall and looked up. Outside there was nothing but dry desert, but in this cave, water dripped down the rocks. I understood why the goddess of water, Anahita, was worshipped here. And why this temple was called Chak Chak: *drip drip*. The atmosphere was mystical, and I let the relentlessly moving crowd take me past the fire tray until I was back outside. I walked back down the couple hundred steps in silence. I was still completely under the spell of that extraordinary place.

When I'd gotten back on my bike and was about to ride off, two young Iranian women walked toward me. I had met them on the climb up to the temple, and already went through a photo shoot with their entire family.

"Hey," I said when I saw them.

"Come with me, lunch," suggested one of the women, wearing a green coat and checked hijab.

"I'm going to Meybod," I said.

She hummed approvingly, patted my arm a few times and said: "Have fun, have fun."

Meybod was the last place around Yazd that I wanted to visit. When I rode into the city, I had a brief moment of déjà vu: the narrow alleyways and mud-brick houses looked exactly like those in Yazd. I turned into one of the alleyways, hoping to end up at the famous Narin castle. But what had started out as an alleyway suddenly turned into a narrow tunnel. The tunnel turned sharply to the right, and I carefully tried to look around the corner from the seat of my motorcycle. I had no idea if this was still part of the city, or whether I was in the process of riding into someone's personal basement. I pushed off against the ground with my feet to roll Basanti backward.

"There is a way, you can go there, you can go," I suddenly heard behind me in perfect English. An Iranian man wearing black sunglasses and a beautiful white, traditional shirt rushed toward me.

"Yes? Okay, because I wasn't sure." I laughed.

"There is a way, it will go to the street, next to Narin castle," he explained.

"I'll try that corner, it's a little bit tight that corner, but I'll try."

"No problem," he said. "Have a good time."

I looked ahead again and carefully squeezed through the narrow turns, bike and all. As promised, the tunnel did bring me to the gates of the castle, and I parked in front of its entrance.

I had barely dismounted when two Iranian women approached me again, their hands outstretched toward me. I shook one of their hands and she said: "Thank you!" with a radiant smile.

"How are you?" I asked in Farsi.

"Thank you, thank you," they said elatedly, thrilled to hear me say a few words in their language.

"Hello, how are you?" asked the younger woman in English. Her father came to meet me as well and invited me to join his family for a meal. By then I had lost count of the number of invitations to lunch, dinner, or slumber parties I'd received. Every day, Iranians I had never met before invited me to meet their families and share a meal. It was a kind of hospitality I had never experienced before. I didn't grow up in a country where we invite perfect strangers off the street for dinner. But Iranians viewed it as an honor to be able to welcome a guest in their home, and it was important to them that I had a good experience in their country. The people in Iran were so different from how I had imagined them. I realized just how much my expectations had been shaped by what I'd seen in the news, and that was almost always about the regime and the geopolitical power dynamics in the Middle East. I had heard about foreign tourists who were arrested because they were (unjustly) suspected of espionage, and about women who had received brutal punishments from the morality police for not wearing their hijab (properly). Yes, I definitely had to be careful with the regime in Iran. I wasn't planning to end up in an Iranian cell. But this had subconsciously colored my view of the entire country, even though I knew that a regime was usually not representative of the population itself. Even in democracies, there are times when leaders are elected that leave you wondering how on earth they might have been chosen.

It was here in Iran that I realized for the first time that my journey wasn't just about me anymore. When I trekked around the world with a backpack in my mid-twenties, I did it for myself. Goofing off and being a full-time tourist—that's what I had experimented with extensively. But I was no longer interested in that.

Now I was trying to make traveling my job. But even more than that, I wanted to create and tell visual stories about people and places that not everyone knew. Show a side to the world I saw every day, but that was often snowed under by all the negative stories, wars, and misery. Even armed with just a small camera on my helmet, I had the opportunity to show others what people were really like in a country such as Iran. And that they were not people that we had to fear.

Chapter 6

To the Lions

Miles: 9,260

For the first few weeks of my motorcycle adventure, as I rode through India and Myanmar, I was so exhausted each day that I was usually out cold by 8 p.m., sleeping for ten hours or more easily. Gradually, though, I started to notice that I could cover longer distances in less time and would arrive at my destination feeling less depleted. As the months passed, the pain from my seat, the shoulder soreness, and all the other discomforts of riding for hours gradually faded into the background. I got used to life in the saddle.

But even though I could ride for longer stretches, I still had to stop constantly in Iran—because of the countless checkpoints. It never became fully clear to me what it was they were checking for, but more or less the same thing happened at every one of them.

It went like this: a man in a dark blue uniform who had seen me approaching picked me out of the line.

"Hi," I said, lifting the visor of my helmet.

"Hi," he said, looking surprised at his own use of the English word.

"*Khubi,*" I said. *How are you.*

"Do you speak Farsi?"

I shook my head. "Holland."

A second man, also wearing a dark blue uniform, came to see what was going on and asked: "Woman?"

"Yes," I replied.

They looked as if they had their own thoughts about that, but it was the only answer I could give them.

"*Show haret kojas,*" uniform two said, laughing. *Where is your husband?*

I didn't plan on explaining to the man in uniform, no matter what kind of authority he worked for, why I wasn't married. I said nothing. By now man number three in uniform had joined the group, and the three of them studied me for a while.

Then number two suddenly said: "Go."

I figured that to be an excellent idea, and they saw me off laughing with a thumbs-up and an "Okay!"

—

After Yazd, I rode to the larger city Esfahan and immediately got myself settled in a hostel, planning to explore every nook and cranny of the city. There was so much to see. The immense Naqsh-e Jahan Square with the Imam Khomeini Mosque, the Ali Qapu Palace, the Vank Cathedral, the old bridges over the Zayandeh River. There were historic bathhouses, bazaars, palaces, and hundreds of restaurants. I pictured myself wandering the city for days and fully immersing myself in ancient Persia. But that never happened.

On the first day, I stepped out of the hostel dressed meticulously in my only pair of jeans, a long shirt with long sleeves, and my scarf that doubled as a hijab. To my mind, my outfit was perfectly proper and not at all too revealing or provocative. But I was still immediately and relentlessly harassed by young men in cars. They honked, yelled, hissed, and whistled at me. I couldn't take ten steps without another one shouting something, gesturing, or making inappropriate noises at me.

I had no clue what was going on. On my motorcycle, I had been treated with respect, often even with admiration and awe. I was invited to meals and welcomed everywhere in the country. But on foot, it was like I had lost my hero's cape and gone back to just being a woman alone on the street, who had to be reminded of her place. The harassment was so overwhelming that it wasn't innocent or funny but intimidating. I rushed back to the hostel and left the city without seeing any of the sights. Iran had completely surprised me for a second time. First it had welcomed me with open arms, only to let me go and hurl me to the lions. Maybe I'd simply been unlucky and run into the exact sort of riled-up youth that felt like having a bit of fun at my expense. I convinced myself that the hissing, catcalling men hadn't *really* been a threat, but it nonetheless took me some time to be able to enjoy Iran's beauty again.

I rode to Kashan in the rain, and to the Iranian capital Teheran in even more rain. There, I occupied myself only with attempting to pick up my visa for neighboring Turkmenistan (which failed) and arranging for a small maintenance service for Basanti (which succeeded). I didn't relax until I left those cities behind and finally reached the Alborz Mountains. Maybe it had just been the city folk. Their reputation of being less friendly than their rural counterparts—the villagers—didn't come from nothing.

–

That things would go south so quickly in the Alborz, and that I would have to abandon my broken-down motorcycle on that steep mountain, losing my mode of transportation and an eyebrow in the process, was something I hadn't counted on. After we'd pushed Basanti to the elderly couple's house and I had freshened up in their bathroom, I was given a hot cup of tea and freshly baked, soft Iranian bread. That night, my belly warm and full, I fell into a deep sleep on the thin mattress they had laid out for me on the rug.

I was woken up early by an unforgiving rooster crowing directly under my bedroom window. I turned onto my stomach and stayed on the floor mattress for a little longer. I had been thinking about a plan from the moment I'd left Basanti behind. I still didn't know much about motorcycle mechanics, but the only thing I could come up with was that there was a problem with my clutch. When I released the clutch lever, nothing happened—but the engine didn't stall either. The clutch cable was faulty, that had to be it. I thought back to the lessons I'd received in Karol Bagh and tried to recall the steps to replace this cable. It hadn't seemed very difficult at the time, and I hoped I still remembered how to do it.

I stretched and got up. I brushed my hair and quickly got dressed. When I stepped into the living room, I was surprised to find a breakfast already waiting for me on a tray. Fried eggs, chunks of fresh bread, and a cup of tea. We hadn't properly introduced ourselves until late the previous night. The married couple were named Shams Ali and Sakineh, and their grandsons were Erfan and the younger Abolfazl.

Sakineh sat cross-legged in front of me and watched with a motherly satisfaction as I greedily wolfed down my breakfast. I wiped my plate clean with the last piece of bread and smiled at Sakineh with a full mouth. She returned my smile with her eyes and pointed at the front door.

"Shams Ali," she said.

I nodded and stood up. When I opened the door, I briefly blinked in the light. The sun shone above the green fields, and it was only now that I realized how lucky I'd been to find this house. I put on my boots and stepped into the garden. Shams Ali and Erfan were busy washing the mud off Basanti. Shams Ali was holding a garden hose and Abolfazl was furiously polishing the rims with a rag. I watched them for a while, from a distance, and as I stood there with a stupid grin on my face, my heart overflowed with the love this family showed each other—and me. Without having to say anything, they had understood how much my motorcycle meant to me and decided to wash her, unasked, like it was the normal thing to do for a stranger.

With my bike now scrubbed clean, it was my turn to get to work. I opened Basanti's side pannier with a small key and produced the spare clutch cable I'd been carrying for just such an occasion.

"Look," I said triumphantly to Shams Ali and Erfan, who curiously looked on. I bent over the motorcycle and studied the route of the cable. I started by following the broken cable as a guide and pulled the new one alongside it. I took my small bundle of tools from under my seat and opened it. With pursed lips, I examined its contents, refreshing my memory of what on earth was inside. I was aware of Shams Ali's and Erfan's eyes on me, and it felt as though I had to look like I knew what I was doing.

After twenty minutes of fiddling and fidgeting, I looked up from the bike and smiled at Shams Ali. "Done," I said, giving a thumbs-up. He looked at me happily and exclaimed something in Farsi.

I went into the house to collect my things and tie them onto Basanti's back again. I had felt welcome and at home here, but nevertheless I was itching to get back on the road. I was always keenly aware of the limits of hospitality and made sure never to stay somewhere my presence might not be wanted for too long. The trick was to announce your departure well before that point.

I expertly pulled my helmet over my hijab and swung my leg over the motorcycle. With my engine running, I looked at Sakineh, Erfan, and Abolfazl, who had come to see me off.

"Khoda hafez," I shouted, meaning literally "May God keep you safe" but also "Goodbye."

"Khoda hafez," they each shouted in turn. Sakineh quickly grabbed my hand and we both gently squeezed each other's palms. Abolfazl shook my hand too and Erfan said in hesitant but clear English: "Next year!"

"Next year," I said back.

"Inshallah." God willing.

"Inshallah," I repeated.

The night before, while Sakineh had been preparing the tea and bread, we had tried to talk for a while. Erfan spoke a little bit of English, and I had a pocket dictionary of Farsi words and phrases with me. But despite our fervent attempts, we hadn't gotten very far. I would have loved to have gotten to know them better, but the language barrier stood between us like an impassable swamp. All I had understood from Erfan was that he wanted to go to university, but that there wasn't enough money. Both boys' parents had passed away, and that's why they lived with their grandparents. I didn't have much Iranian money, but I always carried a stash of American dollars in case of emergency. With great efforts of persuasion, I had managed to press 150 dollars into Shams Ali's hands. At first, he had explicitly declined, but when I made it clear it was for Erfan's studies, they eventually accepted the money.

Shams Ali insisted on escorting me to the start of the main road, leading the way in his old white car. And yet, even before we made it to the end of the path leading up to their house, I could already tell that the clutch was still not working properly. I was moving, sure, but I knew that something wasn't right. It gave me an uneasy feeling; my mouth went dry. If it wasn't the clutch cable, I couldn't imagine what else might be going on. Had I not replaced the cable correctly after all? I realized at this point that I was more likely to noodle out the recipe for the elixir of life than find out what was going on with my motorcycle. We reached the main road, where Shams Ali pulled over and got out.

"Khoda hafez, khoda hafez," he exclaimed, vigorously shaking my hand. He laughed. It was a relaxed laugh that formed soft lines in his cheeks. *"Khoda posht o panahet,"* he said, pointing at the sky. May God

protect and save you. Then his enormous grin melted into a worried frown. *"Arram, arram,"* and with his hands he mimicked an imaginary handlebar. *Ride slowly*, he instructed me.

All I wanted in that moment was to give him a hug, but I didn't know if that would be okay to do here in public. Instead I smiled, said goodbye, and rode away. The euphoria I'd felt just that morning, when I'd managed to replace the clutch cable myself, had completely disappeared. Basanti was still broken and I had no idea what the problem was or where I'd be able to find a mechanic who could repair her. At first, I was going fifty miles an hour, but I couldn't upshift any longer, and my speed fell to forty, then twenty-five and eventually all I could manage was a measly twenty miles an hour in first gear. I crawled along the road at a snail's pace while the engine revved at high rpm, making a ton of noise.

"This is not good, this is not good," I muttered.

As long as I was still moving, I hoped I'd be able to reach a nearby town called Sari. Maybe I could find a mechanic there who could fix my problem with the clutch cable once and for all. Then I saw a small building on the side of the road with lots of car tires stacked outside. I instinctively slowed down. Car tires meant a mechanic. Hopefully they also knew a thing or two about motorcycles. I came to a stop and immediately addressed a man standing by the tires.

"Problem, problem," I said, despair in my eyes. How it happened exactly was a mystery to me, but a few minutes later an entire crowd had gathered. People were rapidly talking into their phones and calling friends. I just stood there a little bewildered, unsure of what to do.

"He has a shop, he sells motorcycle parts, okay," said a man with an oval face and a close-cropped haircut, pointing at one of the other assembled men. He had a deep voice and his English had a beautiful, gentle accent. "It's no problem," he said. "Don't worry, because he can do it, he can do it," he assured me once more.

"The clutch cable is busted," I said, shrugging my shoulders. "I don't understand why it keeps breaking. I replaced it just this morning."

The owner of the motorcycle shop, whose name turned out to be Hamed, gestured for me to step aside and nimbly swung his leg over Basanti. He started the engine, rode about thirty feet and immediately turned around. He said something to the man with the oval face, who translated the message.

"It's the clutch plates."

I shook my head. "No, no, it's the clutch cable." I had been in my own company for too long, with many hours to convince myself of what the problem was. My confusion involuntarily presented itself as frustration, in my frown and my voice.

"Clutch plates, one hundred percent," he said again.

Meanwhile, a number of bystanders were pushing and shoving each other aside to be the one to lift Basanti into the bed of a pickup truck. The eight lucky ones who had secured themselves a spot around the motorcycle had her up in the blink of an eye, as if she weighed forty pounds instead of 440. The pickup's tailgate had to lay flat; at that position the rear wheel could just about rest on it. We had no ropes or ratchet straps with which to tie Basanti down, so one of the men climbed onto her. His wide smile made his round head even rounder. He sat there like an emperor as we raced to the next village over, where Hamed's motorcycle shop was. I was in the passenger seat of his car; with a mixture of happiness and concern, I watched Basanti hop at every bump, as if she were gleefully enjoying the ride.

It wasn't long before the pickup screeched to a halt in front of a concrete building with a gray, steel, closed door. *Today is Friday*, I suddenly realized. On Friday, all shops in Iran are closed. But with a triumphant grin, Hamed unlocked the door and pulled it open.

The motorcycle shop was the size of a shoebox. It was nothing more than a concrete floor and brick walls with some globs of putty hurled at them in a couple of places. Along the walls lay a small stack of motorcycle tires, a few large jerrycans, some extension cords, and a toolbox. The men rolled Basanti inside and got to work right away. There was barely enough space for two people in the room, so the rest of the party stayed outside. First, Hamed drained the oil and then he opened the side of the engine. I crouched beside him and tried to memorize the different steps of what he did.

When the clutch plates finally came out, Hamed let out a yelp. He shouted something at his friends, who jostled to gawk at the blackened clutch assembly. My clutch plates were so horrifically burned that I wondered if I might be able to auction them off as abstract art.

Hamed gave me an accusatory look, melodramatically shook his head and mumbled something. I cast down my eyes, ashamed of what I'd done.

The man with the oval head, whose name I didn't know, called me and I looked up. "Why do you do this," he asked. "Alone, traveling the world?"

The question felt genuine, and without judgment. I could tell him some story about the profoundness of a journey around the world and how enriching it all was. But in that moment, it didn't feel true at all. I replied that I did it because I felt like it. That was the only answer I had right then. And after seeing the scorched parts in my engine, even that feeling was hard to find.

"We need a completely new clutch, but obviously we don't have one for your motorcycle here," he said.

I hurriedly stood up and replied: "But I have one with me." I opened Basanti's pannier and, after some digging, didn't just produce new clutch plates, but an entire clutch assembly. Hamed stared at me in disbelief. In Delhi, I'd been repeatedly declared a fool for insisting on taking that heavy contraption with me. But now my distrust of Royal Enfield, and my unshakable trust in my own capacity for destruction, turned out to be my salvation.

Hamed snatched the assembly out of my hands, and within ten minutes he'd installed it in the engine and poured the old engine oil back in.

"Change the oil as soon as possible, because this might contain particles of the clutch. I don't have motor oil here, otherwise I would have changed it for you," the oval-face man translated for Hamed.

I nodded. "I will," I assured him.

His serious expression gave way to a smile. "And now, you're coming with us for lunch!"

I agreed and followed Hamed to his house, on a Basanti that once again obediently shifted up when I asked her to. Hamed's wife cooked a number of mouthwatering Iranian dishes and two hours later I said goodbye and traversed the final 19 miles to Sari. I went back to the same hotel where I'd stayed two days before as well, and they gave me the same room.

I finally had time to take care of the blisters on my feet, which I'd sustained during Basanti's rescue mission on the mountain. In two days' time, I hadn't made a single mile of progress, even though I had experienced so much. I was at once tired, disappointed, satisfied, and deeply impressed with Iranians. I didn't know a person could feel that many intense emotions at the same time. Hamed had refused to take money for repairing Basanti. I'd lost count of the number of people who had helped me without question, refusing my offers of payment, and was overcome by a sense of shame. When was the last time I had given a stranger that much help and love without expecting anything in return? I couldn't remember.

My ruminations were interrupted by a text message from the Turkmen embassy. "Hello Muss Noralu," they wrote. "I coll from the embassy Turkm. You visa is ready."

I fist-pumped triumphantly and did a little victory dance in my hotel room. This was amazing news, but it instantly put my plans under pressure. I had wanted to rest in Sari for a few days, to recover from the burned-clutch-mishap. Now that plan had gone up in smoke. If I wanted to reach the Turkmenistan border in time, I didn't have a minute to lose. I had to ride 465 miles to the Iranian city of Mashad, pick up my visa there at the Turkmenistan consulate, and then continue straight on to Turkmenistan.

I looked at my phone and typed in a reply. "I'll see you in two days."

Chapter 7

Secret Service

Miles: 10,780

With my Turkmenistan visa in my passport and fresh oil in my engine, I left Mashad, the final city in Iran, for the border with Turkmenistan only two days later. For a while, the road ran along fields of tall grass with grazing cattle, but apart from a few hills the terrain was mostly flat and barren. Luckily, I knew this would change soon enough. To reach the border with Turkmenistan, I had to go through the Kopet-Dag mountains. This mountain range was about 370 miles long and extended from northeast to southwest, parallel to the border between Iran and Turkmenistan. It was positioned between the two countries like a natural barrier. Before long, I was high enough to see patches of snow covering the leeward side of the mountains.

Leaving Iran turned out to be a lot easier than entering, and as soon as my exit documents were stamped, I rode out of the country. Once on Turkmenistan soil, I didn't waste a single moment. I stopped immediately to take off my helmet and pull the hijab off my head. I took a deep breath, as though it had been stuck so tight across my mouth that I hadn't been able to breathe. I felt liberated. I had worn that hijab every day for almost four weeks and had accepted that this was just something women had to do in Iran. I had no intention of risking prison time or getting into other kinds of trouble with the authorities. There had been moments on the whole of my journey where I'd felt rebellious, but not in Iran. There, I dutifully followed all of the clothing rules and regulations. Now that I was removing my hijab, I was overwhelmed by a sense of regained freedom. As if I had been living underwater for four weeks and could finally surface for air.

On the Turkmenistan side of the border, a guard took my papers, turned around without saying a word, and disappeared from sight.

"Here," he said when he came back with my motorcycle's printed-out temporary importation documents.

The ritual of crossing land borders had become predictable in a lot of ways, and yet every one was still a complete surprise. This was the fifth border I'd crossed on Basanti and although I still knew practically nothing about motorcycle mechanics, I felt like an expert on the logistics of traveling with a motorcycle. I wouldn't need the Carnet de Passage any longer after Iran. They wanted nothing to do with the yellow booklet in Central Asia, and I would have to temporarily import Basanti every time. In every country, they asked for the bike's registration documents, my passport, and sometimes my Dutch motorcycle license. Nobody ever asked for that other, expensively begotten, document: my international motorcycle license. Some customs officials went so far as to check my bike's VIN number, but they usually didn't seem too invested in the whole affair. At the border, after the customs formalities, I usually bought a local third-party liability insurance, a SIM card loaded with minutes and data, and exchanged cash with men carrying large stacks of bills who hung around pretty much every border post. Although it was easy to get out of Iran, things were rather different on the Turkmenistan side of the border. There, I was immediately led into a small room with just a table holding a computer and a large map of Turkmenistan on the wall. A man in uniform stood behind the table and pointed at the map.

"You go from here, to here," he said in English with a heavy accent. His voice sounded tired and grumpy. With his index finger, he traced an imaginary line from Ashgabat to Urgench, right on the border with Uzbekistan.

Then, his tone shifted and he snapped: "Not here and not here." He rapped his knuckles on the areas around the coast and inland Turkmenistan. "Where are you going?" he questioned me. For a moment, I felt like I was back in school, in the Netherlands, being sprung with a pop quiz.

"I'm not going anywhere," I replied. "I'm passing through in a straight line. I'm only stopping here," and I pointed at a spot in the middle of the desert. "In Darvaza." I looked at him innocently, trying to convince him that I was telling the truth. That didn't seem to work, so I gave him a smile, which didn't manage to change his expression either. I had no idea what was going through his mind.

"Doctor, go to the doctor," he said out of nowhere. I wasn't sure I'd heard him correctly.

"Doctor?"

"Yes, go now," he barked, and he pointed at the door. I exited the room as I was told. Outside, I looked around until a border guard saw me and pointed at a room two doors down. I strolled over and knocked on the door twice. Moments later, it swung open, and a man in a long white coat appeared in the doorway. The doctor. I suddenly felt like shouting: *I'm not taking off my clothes and I'm not coughing*, but I didn't say anything. With a wave of his arm, he invited me inside. Hesitantly, I followed him in and sat down on a chair across from him. He grabbed a piece of scrap paper.

"Passport number?" he asked.

I showed him my passport and he noted down my details. Then he stood up, bent over the table, and shone a tiny flashlight first in my right eye and then in my left. He looked at both my eyes for a second time and then nodded, satisfied. Apparently, my pupils had given an Oscar-worthy performance. He scribbled something on the piece of paper, handed it to me and said: "Now on to motorcycle inspection."

I walked outside, clutching the paper and baffled by the Turkmenistan medical checkup. I rode Basanti to the next building, where a soldier ordered me to stop. Four other soldiers approached me from behind, forming a semicircle around me. Every one of them was heavily armed, their faces expressionless as they looked at me.

"Grenade? Bomb? AK-47? Automatic weapon?" barked the man who had stopped me.

I stared at him, too dumbfounded to answer. Part of me expected him to burst out laughing, and then we would all slap each other on the back over this bizarre joke. But that didn't happen. They gazed at me silently and weren't laughing.

"No, no," I stammered. What on earth did they take me for?

The soldier mumbled something, then pointed to the next building. Moving on seemed like a good idea to me. I quickly started the engine and left the soldiers behind. Finally, after one last checkpoint where my passport was studied yet again, I was allowed into Turkmenistan. The border guard hastily added that I was absolutely prohibited from taking any pictures during the first 15 miles. I promised I wouldn't and pulled away. He said it in such a secretive tone that I expected to pass military bases for miles. Or a launchpad for a rocket. Or that, at the very least, I would pass some sort of mysterious construction. But I didn't see anything apart from the insanely gorgeous mountains and the smoothest asphalt I'd come across since Dubai. The pristine Kopet-Dag mountains stretched out in front of me, until I eventually rode into Ashgabat, the capital of Turkmenistan.

–

The highway leading into the city was a wide six-lane road that was completely deserted. Apart from me, there was no other vehicle in sight. For a moment, I started to suspect that I'd missed the zombie apocalypse until I saw a few people standing by the side of the road. My gaze fell on the brooms they were holding. To my surprise, they were busy sweeping the highway—with perfectly even strokes. I blinked. Had I seen that right? I saw a couple more a little farther down the road. They were standing in the middle of the highway with their brooms, barely even looking up as I passed them. To their credit, the highway did look magnificently clean.

I felt my jaw drop slowly when the skyline of the city emerged ahead of me in the distance. Ashgabat consisted exclusively of white marble buildings. Decorative accents were solely done with gold. I rode through deserted streets, past tall, majestic marble buildings, white-gold street lanterns, and temples topped with gold domes. It wasn't only the universities, institutes, and museums that were built with white marble; the apartment buildings, bus stations, underground pedestrian tunnels, and even the fountains in the parks were too. A large portion of this marble was mined in the Kopet-Dag mountains and I wondered if it may have been the marble quarries the border guard hadn't wanted me to photograph.

On the rare occasion that I did see a car, it was white too. Only white cars were allowed into the city and I had heard tales of parking lots full of colored cars outside Ashgabat's city boundaries. There were even rules against driving dirty cars. Inspections took place regularly and citizens who were caught driving a dirty car were fined.

I glanced down at the filthy—but thankfully white—Basanti beneath me and hoped I wouldn't get a fine myself.

The then president of Turkmenistan, Gurbanguly Berdymukhamedov, had been in power since 2007. Remarkably, he was quite the mild dictator, at least compared to his predecessor. He'd been a dentist before he became president and had even written a book on dentistry. His background in the pristine, clinical world of medicine had at first seemed like the only logical explanation for how a city as wacky as Ashgabat could have ever been built. But it turned out to have been his predecessor, Saparmurat Niyazov, who was mostly responsible. Niyazov was the first president of Turkmenistan after its independence from the Soviet Union in 1991. It was under his leadership that Ashgabat's large-scale, white marble construction projects had been executed. He was also responsible for the remarkably bizarre rules in the city, most of which were still enforced. In addition to the ban on non-white cars, there were also bans on gold teeth, long hair, beards and mustaches for men. He closed libraries and banned the opera, circus, ballet, and keeping dogs as pets. He renamed the months and days of the week after cultural and historical Turkmenistan terms. Religious expression was limited to, for example, wearing traditional Islamic attire. There was almost no doubt that this man must have suffered from a serious personality disorder because he had portraits of himself hung everywhere across the city. There were also gold statues of himself all around the country that revolved during the day so that they always faced the sun. The population was obligated to call him *Turkmenbashi*, which means "Leader of All the Turkmen." A city by the Caspian Sea was renamed to carry his name.

Berdymukhamedov came into power when Niyazov died in 2006. He may have been slightly more moderate, but I saw his portrait everywhere too. He had an immaculate haircut, with an arrow-straight side part and thick black eyebrows. He didn't have a beard or a mustache, and as far as I could tell from the portraits, no gold teeth either. It seemed the country's considerable wealth, earned through its enormous oil and gas reserves, was spent hanging ten-foot-tall portraits of the president. Less than an hour ago, I had felt so liberated when I was finally able to take off that hijab. Paradoxically enough, I had then plunged myself into a country led with an iron fist by a mad dictator, where freedom was restricted in completely new and confounding ways.

–

I found a hotel, but by the next morning, I was already itching to leave Ashgabat. My transit visa was valid for five days, and it would theoretically only take me two days to cross the country, but I didn't want to stay in the city any longer than I needed to. It gave me an uncomfortable feeling that I couldn't quite put my finger on. As if I could get arrested at any moment because Basanti wasn't clean enough. Or because I was carrying a book with me. The audacity! Or because they didn't like the look of my face, I don't know. In a city with such bizarre rules, nothing would have even surprised me.

I dragged my luggage down the stairs of the hotel and rode out of Ashgabat, straight into the desert. I could still see the high-rises in my rearview mirror when I got caught in a police trap. The officer, wearing a blindingly white shirt and a formal hat, gestured furiously for me to stop. When I came to a halt, he approached me with a speed gun. He pointed first at the traffic sign that indicated forty kilometers per hour and then showed me the gun's screen. It said sixty-two.

"But I wasn't going that fast," I said in English. His reply was in Russian. Or perhaps it was in Turkmen. "Besides, how do I know that that was my speed, and not someone else's," I continued. I was pretty confident I hadn't broken the speed limit.

The conversation continued like that for a while, with me speaking English and him responding in a language I didn't understand. Eventually I went silent and just looked at him. We had reached a stalemate. He looked back at me in silence before eventually letting me through with an irritated wave.

Soon enough, small sand dunes started appearing along the side of the road, which in some places spilled over onto the asphalt a little. Where did those lovely people who kept the road clean with their brooms go? Just like in Ashgabat, I saw almost no traffic on the road. By now, I was seriously beginning to wonder where the people of Turkmenistan did in fact live. I hadn't seen them in Ashgabat nor in the desert, even though there were supposedly six million of them walking around somewhere.

I had left Ashgabat without breakfast that morning and rode nearly 200 miles before I finally found a restaurant that was open. I stepped into the yellow building, helmet in hand, and was enthusiastically greeted by the restaurant's owner. There, I stuffed myself with tea and chunks of fresh bread until I could take no more. But I hadn't just stopped for food. More so, I was looking for a guide. The famous Darvaza Crater was only about 5 miles into the sandy dunes from the restaurant, but it wasn't easy to find thanks to all the different tracks in the sand. The owner of the restaurant called someone for me straightaway. After a brief conversation, he said in Russian: "Twenty minutes." I paid him the equivalent of $16.50 for the service, and before long, a white station wagon showed up—as promised—to show me the way. I followed the two men in the car through the dunes until they stopped on top of a hill. There it was, down below: an enormous crater, and near it several tents and yurts.

That night, I slept in one of the small tents beside the crater. Before I went to sleep, I walked over and stared at it in wonder for a while. It was a gigantic, gaping hole with a diameter of more than 230 feet and a depth of about 65 feet. The hole is also known as the "Gates of Hell," and I could understand why. If there was ever such a thing as a fiery hell, it must look something like this. The crater was formed accidently in 1971, while Soviet geologists were drilling in this location, exploring for gas. During drilling, the surface collapsed, creating the sinkhole. The geologists noticed natural gas coming out of the crater and in an attempt to prevent the spread of toxic methane, they decided to burn it off. What they didn't anticipate was the fire being fed by subterranean gas, causing the fire to still be burning, more than fifty years later. The flames gave off an orange glow that lit up the black night, dancing. I struggled to tear my gaze away from it. There I was, in the middle of the Turkmen desert, in the dark, by myself, next to a monstrous hellfire.

–

The next morning, I woke up with a swollen face, which is something that always happens to me when I sleep in a tent. I examined my face with the small mirror I carried with me and frowned. It felt like it was still early, but the sun had started to rise and the rays of light on the tent had woken me up. Still under the blanket and half lying, half sitting, I tried to apply mascara. That wasn't easy with swollen eyes, and I ended up with more mascara on my eyelids than my eyelashes. I tried to salvage my face as well as I could with a Q-tip, but eventually, I just got out of the tent. I found myself next to the Gates of Hell, for crying out loud, and all I was doing was worrying about mascara. Big deal. Still, it was something I'd done faithfully since I was fourteen. No, I wouldn't take a step outside without mascara on. It had been part of my daily routine for decades, but now that I was here, in such an alien place, even my most normal of habits felt out of place too.

I decided to hurry up and leave so I could cross the border to Uzbekistan that same day. Somehow, Turkmenistan didn't feel like the kind of country to take your time rolling through. Besides, I had been forbidden from exploring freely. The men at the border hadn't made any attempt to hide their displeasure with me—they couldn't wait to see my backside on its way out of their country.

I found my way back across the sandy tracks without much effort and got back onto the paved road. The entire way was hardly mind-blowing. I saw sand, the pavement, sand, and more pavement. When I thought about the meaning of monotony, this landscape came to mind. Occasionally I would encounter shepherds with camels or see a herd of cows, but that was about it. My entrance into Turkmenistan had been spectacular, with the surreal world of Ashgabat, but now it felt like the city had spat me out into the dull, vast desert.

Finally, after a long day's ride, I spotted a fence and a soldier in the distance and took a relieved breath. I had arrived at the border with Uzbekistan.

A humongous portrait of the ever present Berdymukhamedov hung above the border office of Turkmenistan, and I looked at it one last time. *Goodbye, Mr. President, without beard, mustache, or gold teeth,* I thought. Then the process of leaving Turkmenistan began, which rivaled the bizarre scenes of my entrance. I was sent to another doctor, though this one was utterly uninterested in my pupils. Instead, he pointed a gun-shaped device at my forehead and pulled the trigger. He looked at the reading and wrote 37.5 on a form. He seemed satisfied with that result and sent me away. I wondered what they would have done with me if I'd had a fever, but I didn't have much time to think about that. As soon as I exited the doctor's office with the form in my hand, another man in uniform was already beckoning me. He led me into the next room and pointed at a chair. I sat down. Two government employees looked me right in the eye, and one of them said: "Give the GPS tracker." His nose ran straight down the center of a symmetrical, powerful face and flowed into tight, thin lips.

I looked at him with raised eyebrows. "GPS tracker?"

"GPS tracker."

"I don't have a GPS tracker," I replied.

"Yes, you do. Give it back." His voice had gained a sharp undertone.

"No, I don't have one."

"Yes you do, give now." I didn't understand what on earth they were talking about. What GPS tracker? Were they talking about my phone?

"My phone?" I asked, holding it up.

"No, G-P-S tracker," the government employee screamed, as if I was an imbecile. Perhaps I was, but that was no excuse for him to scream at me like that. The man gave me a furious look and grabbed the receiver of the landline sitting on the table next to him.

"Border Iran, they give you," he said while putting the phone to his ear.

"No, they didn't," I squeaked. "I never got a GPS tracker at the border."

He dialed a number and looked away. As he did, I studied his face. Did he work for Turkmenistan's secret service? Why else would they be asking for a GPS tracker? After the phone had rung a couple of times, somebody picked up and the man began to talk rapidly. I just sat there in my chair, nervously wringing my hands. I didn't know how I could prove that they had never given me a GPS tracker. It hadn't even been necessary, I thought, because I had dutifully followed their instructions and ridden in a straight line through the country. I hadn't been bold enough to ride to the coastal areas even out of spite.

After talking busily for a while, the man slammed down the phone. "Just go, just go," was all he said.

–

It was thankfully a lot easier to get into Uzbekistan, and there were no doctors looking at my pupils or soldiers questioning me about potential bombs and grenades in my possession. The Uzbekistani desert resembled the one from Turkmenistan: flat and monotonous. But the cities were completely different. Instead of white marble, the buildings here were made of mud. Their earthy tones were complemented with mosaics, decorative tiles, and intricately detailed wood carvings. Their mosques had blue domes and were built from stunning brickwork.

I spent a few days in Khiva, a place once founded as an oasis along the Silk Road. For centuries, it was the main trading route for transporting precious silk to the west. Now, Khiva was a historic city brimming with old palaces, minarets, and madrassas (Islamic schools). Uzbekistan had a rich diversity of ethnic groups. Although the majority was Uzbek and spoke the Uzbek language, Tajiks, Tatars, Karakalpaks, Kurds, Russians, and Kazakhs lived there too. I rented a room in a family home in the center of the city and the women in the house all looked beautiful. They wore colorful tunics with lively patterns and embroidery, a matching *duppi* (headscarf) and often a *chachvan*—a short coat with embroidered embellishments. They adorned themselves with bracelets, necklaces, earrings, and rings.

The Uzbeks were keen to chat with me, and we tried to have short conversations in a combination of Russian and English. I was glad to be able to speak to some people again, because in Turkmenistan that had been nearly impossible. With only the occasional exception, I'd always felt a certain distance—as though they were afraid to talk to me. Maybe it had been thanks to the camera on my helmet, which made me look like a journalist. I could imagine that journalists weren't quite the popular kids in Turkmenistan.

After leaving Khiva, I wrestled my way through a flat desert for hundreds of miles. Although I couldn't see them yet, I knew they were there in the distance: the mountains of Tajikistan. They had a magnetic attraction over me and I would have skipped the flat emptiness in one big hopscotch if only I could. Strangely enough, mountains have always had that effect on me, despite being born in just about the flattest country in the world. What am I saying—I was born twenty feet *below* sea level. It doesn't get much lower than that. Perhaps that was the reason for my fascination with mountains.

Uzbekistan turned out to be a horrible country for Basanti. The Uzbek gas had low octane levels that was often contaminated with water or dirt. I also needed to arrange an oil change, but new engine oil was impossible to find, no matter how many Uzbeks I asked. The only oil for sale was meant for cars, and I didn't dare to risk sticking that in my engine. I could have sworn I heard Basanti cough every once in a while, because of the bad fuel and lack of clean oil. I became so paranoid that

I took to lowering my head while riding, until it was right above the tank, listening for strange noises. Did the engine sound different than normal, or was I imagining it? Usually, I was able to convince myself that everything was fine, only to hear another strange gurgle giving me the heebie-jeebies. There was no motorcycle mechanic or dealership to be found in Uzbekistan, and my first chance at getting oil wouldn't be until Tajikistan's capital, Dushanbe. All I could do was pretend I didn't hear anything out of the ordinary. Occasionally, ostrich-ing is the only way to keep going.

Most days, I ate salty rice porridge and greasy puff pastries for breakfast. For both lunch and dinner, there was a choice of two dishes: *laghman* or *plov*. The *laghman* was thick noodles mixed with bits of meat and sometimes a few vegetables and was actually a typical Uyghur dish. *Plov* was the national dish of Uzbekistan, consisting of rice pilaf stewed with pieces of lamb's meat. I tore through my first few plates of *plov* like a hungry animal, but I was ready to hurl after eating nothing else for days on end. I yearned for the moist, freshly baked bread and endless variation of dishes in Iran. My taste buds cried for the creamy hummus, spicy kebabs, and the bright-red, flavorful tomatoes in those dishes. It was hard to believe a mere two countries over, the explosions of flavor from the Persian cuisine had been replaced by greasy puff pastries and *plov*. Thanks to the unattractive desert, the boring food, the lack of engine oil, and the bad gas, my mood had plummeted to absolute zero. I realized Uzbekistan wasn't for me.

The last big city before the border with Tajikistan was Samarkand, and I planned to immediately push through to the snowcapped mountains that had been calling me all along. But when I rode into Samarkand and saw its imposing buildings, I decided to give Uzbekistan one last chance. In a way, it felt like I was already in Tajikistan, because Samarkand was mostly inhabited by people of the Tajik ethnicity, and the people around me primarily spoke Tajik. This was because when the Soviet Union was founded in 1924, the Uzbeks and Tajiks had initially been united under the Uzbek Soviet Socialist Republic. It was split up again five years later into a Tajik SSR and an Uzbek SSR, though the Uzbeks retained the Samarkand region. This didn't change even when the Soviet Union collapsed and both countries became independent in 1991.

I wandered from my hostel to the large square I'd spotted as I rode into the city. This was the *registan*, meaning "sandy place" in Persian. Up close, it was even more colossal and impressive than I'd thought, and it turned out to have nothing to do with a sandy place. There were three madrassas on the square. The buildings' interiors were adorned with intricate mosaic decorations and a gold-colored dome ceiling. The entire square exuded culture and history, and I relished the sun on my face as I strolled past the structures in my T-shirt.

I was glad I had stayed in Samarkand for a few days and experienced this completely different side of Uzbekistan. It had taken me by surprise. I might have known in advance that this place was special; there was plenty to read up about it. But I often refrained from doing excessive research into countries, on purpose. I didn't want to know everything beforehand. That would only raise my expectations, and inevitably lead to disappointment. I'd rather be surprised, and Uzbekistan had managed to do just that.

It also turned out to be the last warm day for the foreseeable future. When I left Samarkand the next morning, it was suddenly a lot colder and raining incessantly. The weather didn't bother me much, because once I'd crossed the border and ridden into Tajikistan, I finally reached the mountains I had been looking forward to for so long. After those endless, dull deserts, I reveled in the rugged mountain peaks, rivers, sweeping green valleys, and clusters of trees scattered throughout. There was still quite a bit of snow on the mountaintops, and I noticed that the road was slowly starting to climb. It wasn't long before I reached the Anzob Tunnel, also known as the "tunnel of death." A soldier stood outside the entrance to the tunnel, gesturing for me to pull over. I came to a stop right in front of him and switched off the engine. He wore a blue camouflage suit with matching cap and had a long rifle slung over his shoulder. He said something in Russian I didn't understand.

"How many kilometers," I asked in English. He held up a hand with the fingers splayed.

"Five?" I said, switching back to Russian.

Pyat.

"Five. Three," he said.

I took that to mean that the tunnel was 5.3 kilometers long.

"Yes," he said again, glancing at my bike, then adding something that ended with "lampa." I quickly turned my key in the ignition, turned on my high beams and pressed the red button to activate my two additional headlights. He nodded, satisfied.

"*Normal*," he said. It was good enough. "Alone, yes?" he asked, holding up one finger. Then he mimed riding a motorcycle and pointed at the road behind me to ask if there were more motorcyclists on the way.

"I'm alone," I said.

He nodded again and suddenly told me to get lost. Or that's what it sounded like, anyway.

I started Basanti and turned sharply back onto the road. The entrance of the tunnel looked like a big black hole and turned out to be exactly that. I looked warily into its depths. I wasn't a huge fan of tunnels, not since that one time I went through the Heinenoord Tunnel.

–

I grew up on an island. A big island, sure, but an island all the same. My high school was 12.5 miles away, in the same town where all of my classmates lived. While they walked or cycled to school, I had to take the bus. An hour on the 164 regional bus, which snaked its way passed the other towns on the island. Next, a transfer at the Heinenoord bus station and onward on the 267. This second bus left the island through the Heinenoord Tunnel, and on the other side of the water, it went directly to Barendrecht, a larger town under the smoke of Rotterdam, where I went to school.

I used to take the bus with a friend from down the street, but because I took Latin and classical Greek classes, I soon had to start going to the campus in Rotterdam. Away from Barendrecht and on to the big city.

One day, when I was fourteen, I figured I could just ride my Rollerblades to Rotterdam instead of taking the bus. *It isn't* that *far*, I thought. Only I hadn't considered that 12.5 miles on tiny Rollerblade wheels may as well have been an intergalactic odyssey. It felt like the journey would never end, and I'd failed to take the tunnel into account, even though I had traveled through it twice a day on the bus. On my Rollerblades, I had to take the special tractor tunnel, which went down and then up at a much steeper angle than the main tunnel. Without peeking into the tunnel hole first, I skated right over the edge. Before I knew it, I was whizzing straight down at breakneck speed, as

I desperately strained to keep my knees slightly bent. A warm, musty wind in the tunnel invaded my nostrils, making my eyes itch.

Suddenly, I saw an obstacle ahead. What was it? A kind of grate? A concrete ridge? It was rapidly coming closer, and at the very last second, I jumped. I soared through the air for what felt like an eternity. Then both my Rollerblades slapped back onto the concrete. I hadn't fallen! My heart nearly leaped out of my chest with relief. But I immediately had to pick up speed so I'd have enough momentum to get back up the other side. Huffing, puffing, and red-faced I clawed my way up. With gritted teeth, I kept pushing off with the wheels of my Rollerblades. I was only halfway there. *Keep going. Don't stop.* I made it to the top of the tunnel, and then to school, haggard and sweaty. The first two classmates I told that I'd come to school on my Rollerblades laughed. "You just took the bus and put on your Rollerblades before coming in."

Nobody believed me. I never attempted such a thing again after that.

–

I steered Basanti into the darkness of the Anzob Tunnel. In a sense, I hadn't changed at all since high school: I was still throwing myself into dark tunnels, at full speed toward the unknown.

There was no lighting whatsoever within, and even with Basanti's brights turned on, I could hardly see. Twice, I slammed into deep holes in the road surface that I hadn't spotted. The second time, I hit one so hard that I almost lost my grip on the handlebars. A dense mist of exhaust fumes hung motionless in the tunnel, reflecting the light from my headlights straight back into my eyes. I struggled to breathe. As carefully and at the same time as quickly as I could, I kept going but the tunnel seemed to go on forever. I came across oncoming traffic three times and was completely blinded by their headlights. I had to stop and wait for them to pass to keep from face-planting into the tunnel walls. My eyes had started to lightly water but then, through a haze of tears, exhaust fumes, and darkness, a pinprick of light appeared. It grew bigger and bigger, until the tunnel ejected me out onto the other side.

I blinked, adjusting to the daylight, and was overjoyed to find that I'd ridden into a winter wonderland. The mountains around me were covered in a gorgeous, thick layer of snow. The road was thankfully snow-free, and with a big grin on my face, I rode onward to Dushanbe.

Chapter 8

Pink Slippers

Miles: 11,870

Dushanbe, the capital of Tajikistan, looked completely different from how I'd pictured it. In my imagination, it was a colorless city full of tall, dilapidated Soviet apartment complexes, trash stacked high on the sides of abandoned streets, and sullen-looking people. This wasn't the first time I felt embarrassed with my own uneducated preconceptions.

The city I saw, as I skillfully attempted to navigate Basanti through traffic over brand-new asphalt, was totally different. The buildings definitely were tall, but instead of gray and dilapidated, they were modern and painted in pastel colors. In the middle of the four-lane road, a green island had been constructed with a manicured lawn, tall trees, and even a pergola. The curb was painted in precisely measured sections of yellow and black to indicate that it was a no-stopping or parking zone. I saw Tajik women in long, colorful tunics with matching pants and headscarves walking down the street, not looking even the slightest bit sullen. They strolled casually along the boulevard in the company of their husbands and children. If it wasn't for the fact that I couldn't read any of the Cyrillic texts on the billboards, I might have felt much less far from home than I actually was.

I slowed down and stopped in front of a tall, bright green metal gate. It had a small sign with a pictogram of a house with the text GREEN HOUSE HOSTEL written below it, first in Cyrillic and then in English. Dushanbe had dozens of hostels and hotels, but this hostel had the reputation as the most popular place to spend the night and meet fellow travelers, almost like a small western enclave in the heart of Central Asia. The moment I dismounted to ring the doorbell, the side door opened and a young man appeared. He was wearing a gray cardigan and white socks in slides. With his short beard and round glasses, he had a friendly presence.

"Do you want to park inside?" he called out.

"Yes, please," I replied.

He walked back and I heard him fumbling with the lock on the other side of the steel door. Then the two wide doors swung open. The owners had taken the name of their hostel quite seriously because besides the green steel entrance and the Granny Smith green fencing, all walls in the courtyard had been painted green as well. Two different shades, even. I slowly rolled Basanti inside and parked beside a—what else—green water barrel that had been placed under a small green roof. I didn't see any other motorcycles, just a few mountain bikes.

"Where do you want me to— Is this okay?" I asked, turning my head as far as my helmet would allow.

The young man smiled and nodded.

I climbed off Basanti and briefly stretched my legs. "How are you?" I asked.

"Good, and you?"

"Good." I wondered if I should immediately unleash my worries on him about the state of the road I'd have to take from here. I decided against it and left it at "good."

"I made two bookings—" I began.

"Private room for two nights, right?" he interjected, completing my sentence. Either there weren't many reservations, or he rightly thought that I looked like a Noraly Schoenmaker.

"Yes," I said. "I was delayed, and I wanted to let you know but I didn't have internet."

"I understand, no problem," he said, and he smiled at me.

I untied my large waterproof duffel bag from Basanti and followed him into the hostel, where he led me to a small but neat room. Most of the rooms in the hostel were meant to be shared and had bunk beds in them, but I had opted for a private one.

I'd moved past the point in my life of sharing a room with six random strangers. When I was backpacking in my twenties, I fell into the category "oceans of time, puddles of money." I had a daily budget that I tracked meticulously in notebooks, turning the search for the cheapest accommodation possible into an Olympic sport. With that method, I managed to stay on the road for two and a half years, but that did mean that I had to share a room with a group of strangers on a daily basis. Always a different crowd but never without snorers or smelly feet.

Technically, I still fell into that same category—more time than money on my hands—but I had made the conscious decision to take a different approach this time. I planned to use the money from selling my house and Ducati Monster to pay for this motorcycle trip, until I ran completely dry. I'd decided that if I was still not earning enough with my videos by then, I would have no other choice but to return to the Netherlands and find work again. My philosophy was: when it's gone, it's gone. I simply accepted that I would go broke sooner by booking private rooms. I truly felt too old for dorms.

My two-night reservation turned out to be a touch optimistic. Just as I closed the door to my room behind me, I heard my phone ping. A message appeared from Hafiz, owner of Bike House Dushanbe. I had asked him the day before if I could drop off my bike for a service. I quickly unlocked my phone to read his message and slumped onto the side of the bed, disappointed.

"Hey, Noraly," the message read. "Aziz is our main mechanic and he's in Russia at the moment. He will be here in a few days. I wrote to him, waiting for his reply." Then another message came in. "There is other guys in other bike shops, but they are not reliable honestly."

I believed his statement about the competition. Aziz had been recommended by every other traveler, and I wasn't about to put Basanti in the care of unreliable characters. I quickly typed back: "Okay, if Aziz will be back in a few days, I will wait for him."

I stared at my phone screen, feeling defeated. I had hoped to move on quickly, though admittedly, Hafiz's message had not come as a complete surprise. I knew I got here too early. At this time in the season, the mountain passes were still covered in a thick layer of snow. I had once again covered too much distance in too little time over the past few weeks. This was partially due to my short transit visa for Turkmenistan, but mostly it was because of me. I couldn't help myself, I was too hungry for whatever lay behind the next corner to stay anywhere for long. My friend Mandy and I always joked about this together. While I would tear across a continent like a woman possessed, she could easily spend three months in a small country like Laos. After years of working herself to the bone as a hotel manager, she had finally mastered the art of doing nothing. She could with ease spend an entire afternoon relaxing in a café with a book or by simply watching life go by in a random, Laos village. I could never do that; I always had to stay busy.

–

Once I had wriggled out of my motorcycle clothes and quickly freshened up, I walked downstairs. My stomach was rumbling and, as usual, I didn't have any food with me. I couldn't just swing by Target for a box of granola bars here, I hadn't brought Tupperware to take food for the road, and I definitely didn't have cooking utensils to whip up something myself. This had never been a problem in Southeast Asia because there had always been food stalls and restaurants by the side of the road. Things were very different here, and it took a lot more effort to find something to eat. While I walked across the courtyard toward the gate, I noticed three cyclists had arrived in the meantime. I didn't see them, but their bikes, with carefully fastened bags, were parked next to the mountain bikes. I was always impressed with people traveling the world on a bicycle. They made me realize that, compared to them, what I was doing wasn't all that remarkable. Putting aside the physical demands of traveling the world solely on your own steam, they were also the kings and queens of lightweight travel. And always lugging with them a full set of camping gear, too. With a motorcycle, I never had to resort to camping, because I could easily cover an extra 125 miles to find a roof over my head if I had to. But most cyclists I met covered only between 50 and 60 miles a day, and in many countries the hotels were farther apart than that. For them, camping was unavoidable.

I carried a lot more luggage than they did and didn't even camp. But spare parts for a motorcycle were bigger and heavier than those for a bicycle, right? I took another look at the three bikes. The thought of the conversations I would have with fellow travelers in the next few days cheered me up instantly.

That night, I sat cross-legged at a low table opposite a young Frenchman named Valentin. He owned the bicycle with the red panniers. Two small red bags were tied on either side of his front wheel, two larger red bags to the back, and he had a black bar bag on the front. We shook hands and his gaze had a certain lack of inhibition that immediately endeared me to him. The other bicycles, I learned, belonged to a couple, Alba and Thomas, who were traveling with Valentin for a few days.

I took a good look at Valentin. His face was tanned from months of riding, apart from a white marking where he wore his sunglasses. He had a full head of dark brown hair, a thick beard, and bushy eyebrows. He was a few years younger than me and the unbridled energy with which he talked about his adventures was infectious. With a singsong French accent that I found both charming and occasionally somewhat feminine, he asked when I was leaving Dushanbe.

"Not for a while," I said with a grimace. "My motorcycle needs to be serviced, but the bike shop isn't open yet. It won't be for another five days."

"Good," he replied teasingly. "I'm stuck here for a few days too, waiting for a parcel. At least I'll have company."

I laughed. "I'm afraid I won't be great company," I said. "I have an insane amount of work to do." I told him about the videos I made of my travels, and he jumped up, full of excitement.

"Wait, wait, I have something for you," he exclaimed.

Curious, I followed him with my gaze as he took one of the big red bags off his bicycle and started digging around in it. To my astonishment, he pulled out a small keyboard. He looked at me triumphantly and said: "I can write you a song, for one of your videos!"

I couldn't believe it: He was cycling around the world and had left room in his bag for a portable studio. *Note to self: it's high time I go through my own bags again*, I thought, *and send anything I no longer need back to the Netherlands or give it away.*

Valentin set up his keyboard, opened his laptop, and plugged in a small microphone.

"What are you looking for," he asked, looking at me expectantly.

"Something epic," I replied. "I like music that's a little dramatic, it goes well with mountain scenery. But I don't want it to be too ominous, I'd rather have it on the light side than too heavy." I didn't feel like I could properly put into words what I was looking for, but Valentin nodded and got to work.

Within ten minutes, he'd landed on a melody I subconsciously bobbed my head to. "This is the first layer," he said. "Now we're going to give it more body."

I was impressed with his ability to write music on the spot. "Why did you bring all this with you?" I asked. "I mean, it's supercool, but it's also a lot of extra luggage to have on your bike."

He chuckled. "Yeah, it's a lot of stuff. But this way I can make music when I feel inspired by the scenery I cycle through. I use them for my own videos."

In the following days, as it was bucketing down with rain outside, we continued working on the song together. He would play me demos and I would give feedback. Layer by layer we kept adding to the music. In between music sessions, I edited three videos I'd recorded in Uzbekistan, ate *plov*, *laghman*, and delicious Tajik bread, and the two of us talked about places we dreamed of traveling to.

—

After four days of waiting, Bike House Dushanbe finally opened its doors and I was officially their first customer of the season.

"There's still a lot of snow on the pass," Aziz said, his face serious.

"Yes, I've heard," I answered casually, sounding more confident than I felt. "I'll be fine, it will be another couple of days before I'm there." I focused my attention on my motorcycle and hoped Aziz would do the same.

"She needs an oil change and a new oil filter, but I have the filter with me. I prefer the 15W50 oil, semisynthetic or fully synthetic if you have it." Walking around Basanti, I pointed at the parts that required attention as I listed them. "My air filter needs to be cleaned, my chain needs some grease and she doesn't start very well when it's cold in the morning so I'd like you to check her spark plug. Oh, and her handling's off," I added. I was perfectly capable of doing the air filter and chain maintenance myself by now, but because I had known she'd need a service anyway, I had procrastinated and saved those jobs for Aziz.

Aziz swiftly got my motorcycle on its center stand and started to slowly move the handlebars back and forth. "The steering head bearings are worn," he concluded.

"That's impossible," I replied resolutely. "I replaced them back in Kuala Lumpur, that's only 5,000 miles ago. They can't be busted already," I insisted.

Aziz looked at me. "Here, feel for yourself." He brought my hand to my bike's handlebars. Because she was on the center stand, there was no weight on the front wheel. He slowly moved the handlebars from left to right.

"Here, do you feel that? There's a small notch."

I bit my lip. I felt the notch all too well. That might explain why Basanti for the life of her couldn't get around a corner smoothly. But I couldn't accept that the bearings had worn down so quickly. I knew from the full service in Malaysia how much work it was to replace these bearings, and besides, I didn't have any spares with me. *Stupid, so stupid,* I thought to myself. Ordering the bearings from India would set me back two weeks if I was even lucky. After five days of hanging around in Dushanbe, I'd had enough waiting.

"You can still ride like this, you know," Aziz tried to reassure me when he caught my distress. "It will just be difficult riding off-road because the bike doesn't handle well, but you'll get through the Pamir with it. Don't worry."

What Aziz nonchalantly called "the Pamir" I knew to be one of the most legendary routes in the world. The Pamir Highway had, despite its name, no relation to highways as I knew them. The 750-mile-long road from Dushanbe in Tajikistan to Osh in Kyrgyzstan had once been part of the centuries-old Silk Road. In the thirties, it was modernized by the Soviet Union to aid military movements. Since then, both the quality of the road and the merchandise conveyed along it changed, neither for the better. Instead of silk, it was now used to transport ninety tons of heroin and other contraband from Afghanistan every year. It had earned the route the dubious unofficial name "Heroin Highway."

Although parts of the Pamir Highway were recently renewed with beautifully smooth pavement, other parts very much weren't and it remained one of the most challenging routes in the world. Not only because of the road conditions but also because of its placement at such an enormous altitude, which reached up to fifteen thousand feet. It was like sustainedly riding around on the peaks of the Rocky Mountains. From the Hindu Kush mountains in Afghanistan, the Pamir was the link between the Karakoram mountains in Pakistan all the way to the Himalayas in India. It had a mythical status among adventurers, and seeing as how I was in the area anyway, it had seemed only natural to ride it. But now that I knew I would be tackling it with worn steering head bearings, I was slightly less optimistic.

—

I spent my last evening in Dushanbe with Valentin and his companions, Alba and Thomas. We talked about a terrorist attack on seven cyclists that had taken place barely eighteen months ago. Just outside of Dushanbe, a car had plowed into a group of foreigners and although everyone initially assumed it had been an unfortunate accident, it was soon claimed by IS—Islamic State. Dutchman René Wokke was one of the four fatal victims. Although nothing that tragic had happened in Tajikistan since this incident, cyclists in particular were still nervous. I felt safer on my motorcycle, because despite me riding like a grandma, I could still outpace a car on those potholed roads. The cyclists were more vulnerable, and I involuntarily worried about Valentin.

The subject changed to something lighter, so we wouldn't go to bed on such a heavy note. We discussed what kind of food we hoped to find on the way and how many days everyone would take to get to the border with Kyrgyzstan. We talked about the weather forecast for the coming week and speculated about how bad the road might be. That night, I crawled into bed full of anticipation for the upcoming Pamir adventure.

The next morning, I studied my map again. I wanted to reach the village of Qal'ai Khumb in one day, which was right on the Afghan border. It was a long ride, 220 miles, but Aziz had told me that the majority of the road was paved. He said only the final stretch, where I would be riding parallel to the border with Afghanistan, was in terrible condition. I realized that before I even started on the Pamir Highway, I'd already have to deviate from it. The section of the Pamir Highway up to Qal'ai Khumb was still closed because of heavy snowfall, so I had to take a detour via a more southern route, along the Afghan border. It was a pity, but I had no choice. Valentin had already left. It would take him three days to cover the same distance I had planned for just today.

I quickly folded the map and grabbed my helmet. My luggage was already securely loaded and Basanti was waiting for me in the courtyard. I realized that I was itching to leave. I had gotten so used to covering distance every day over the past few months that five days of not being in the saddle felt like an eternity. I longed to ride.

The friendly young man who had let me in five days earlier (whose name was Morodzhon) once again opened the green steel doors for me.

"Thanks, bye," I shouted from under my helmet, while I rode past him through the doors.

"Good luck," he called after me, but I was already out of earshot. All I heard was Basanti's familiar sound. *Put put put,* she said, and, elated, I rode through the streets of Dushanbe until I'd left the place behind entirely.

It wasn't long before I saw a cyclist with red panniers ahead. I slowed down, and he was looking over his shoulder before I'd even reached him.

"I already thought it was you," said Valentin, and he laughed. I stopped and switched off the engine. "Where are Alba and Thomas?"

"Oh, a bit farther ahead," he replied. "I made a quick stop to buy water."

I looked at him and said nothing for a moment.

Valentin broke the silence and urged me not to move too fast because of the Ak-Baital Pass. At an altitude of 15,272 feet, it was the highest pass on the Pamir highway.

"Don't forget that it may take a few days before the snow is gone there," he said.

I nodded, as if I knew exactly where the Ak-Baital Pass was. "Don't worry, I'll be fine," I assured him.

I secretly liked the thought that if everything went wrong, Valentin would eventually catch up to me. Even if I had to spend days lying helplessly in the snow somewhere, eventually he would appear. In a flash, I saw the whole scenario play out in vivid Technicolor. As I lay there shivering, Valentin would cycle toward me and swoop me onto his bike. With me on his pannier rack, he would then bring me to the nearest village, to safety.

"Good luck," Valentin said while he swung his leg back over his bike to continue cycling.

I was jolted out of my ridiculous daydream and called after him: "You too," as if he needed that.

I started Basanti and honked twice when I passed him. I kept looking in my mirror for a while and watched Valentin grow smaller and smaller, until he disappeared from sight entirely. Unless my delusional bicycle-rescue-mission became reality, I would probably never see him again. It made me feel a bit melancholy, though I'd gotten used to the short-lived friendships that you form when you travel. On the road, it was totally normal to become spontaneously joined at the hip with a group of strangers for a couple of days, sharing the intensity of every experience and emotion with one other, only to go your own way at the next crossroad and never speak again. Occasionally, such an encounter led to a long-term friendship—like the one I had with Mandy, who I met on my first trip in India—but that was rare.

–

With Dushanbe behind me, I rode past fields full of blooming red and yellow flowers. The landscape was hilly and everything was so green that I watched it go by in bewilderment. This was nothing like what I'd thought Tajikistan would look like. The hills were unreal; it was like riding through a Bob Ross painting. Aziz had been right—the road was excellent, and I made plenty of progress in the first hours after my departure. But the closer I got to the Afghan border, the more potholes appeared. At first I barely had to slow down to avoid them, but eventually the road became more hole than road, and I imagined I had to be going about the same speed as Valentin on his bicycle.

I approached a checkpoint and shifted down to first gear.

"Hello," I shouted in my best Russian to the soldier who came walking toward me. I didn't speak a lot of Russian, but "hello" was by far my favorite word. I wasn't sure why—perhaps because it just rolled off the tongue so smoothly. *Zdravstvuyte.* I didn't speak a single word of Tajik, but Russian was still an official language in Tajikistan, so unsurprisingly most Tajiks spoke it much more fluently than I did.

He gestured for me to ride a little farther, past the barrier. I did and then came to a halt.

"Hello," the soldier said to me in English. "Where are you going?"

"To Qal'ai Khumb," I replied, slightly relieved that he spoke English. "Do you need my passport?"

"Passport," he repeated, nodding. I put Basanti on the kickstand and dismounted. "Where are you from?" he asked.

"Holland."

It was a question I got asked every single day. I had learned by now that "The Netherlands" usually didn't ring any bells.

I took out my passport and handed it to the young soldier, who was seemingly still dressed in his winter uniform. He wore a thick camouflage coat with a fur collar, a camouflage hat, camouflage pants with high black combat boots, and a wide belt wrapped around his coat. As I watched him disappear into a small square building with my passport, I was approached by a man in a long black coat. Underneath, he wore a shirt and tie. He had emerged from a new-looking black SUV that was parked nearby. A car like that didn't fit the streetscape of Tajik at all; he was almost certainly a high-ranking government official. Or maybe a secret agent. Either way, he looked like someone who possessed information.

"The road is good, bad, good?" I asked. That was the only kind of information I was interested in.

"Good," said the man, giving me a thumbs-up. I had developed the habit of asking everyone who spoke to me about the road conditions. Sometimes it yielded valuable tips and other times total rubbish. This time his answer fell into the latter category. The stretch of road after the checkpoint had so many potholes that I kept on slamming into them with my front wheel. Perhaps the man had been referring to the road a few miles farther along, because after that section was over, I sped off toward the high mountains on smooth asphalt.

One hundred fifty-five miles after leaving Dushanbe, I finally reached the border with Afghanistan.

At first sight of the mountains on the other side of the Panj river, which marked the countries' border, my breath quickened. After years of only hearing about Afghanistan in the news, almost always as part of bad news, it felt surreal to be here at its outskirts. The mountains were so wild and untamed that I stopped to gaze at them for a while. On the other side of the river ran a narrow, unpaved road, and I wondered what it would be like to ride on it. Would the road on the other side of the river, in Afghanistan, feel somehow different than on this side in Tajikistan?

After having ridden south since Dushanbe, I now turned toward the east. I had to follow the border with Afghanistan for another 60 miles to reach Qal'ai Khumb. The gorge I rode through got narrower and narrower the farther I went, all the while passing waterfalls. Sometimes, I passed through a small village with white-painted houses and cone-shaped roofs, and other times I saw a village across the river, on Afghanistan's side. Those villages mostly consisted of mud houses with flat roofs. Apricot trees grew on the edges of the Tajik villages and I saw fields of wheat, barley, and peas. The green of the crops contrasted with the barren, steep mountainsides around them. I smiled at the children that invariably stood by the side of the road in every village to wave at me. The sound of Basanti's exhaust echoed through the gorge and made the children run toward me like I was the pied piper.

"Hello," I called out while I slowed to a stop in one of the villages. A troop of kids flocked around me. The children were always the first to welcome me, they weren't afraid. As children we fear the dark, monsters under the bed, and thunderstorms, but not each other. We don't learn to fear each other until later.

"What's your name?" a little boy asked in English after I shook his hand.

"Noraly," I replied. "And what's yours?"

"My name is Ruto," he replied, before timidly putting his hand in his pocket.

"Wow, what a nice name," I said while shaking the hand of a little boy wearing a Gucci sweater. The Gucci boy asked for my name too.

"Noraly. What's your name?"

"My name is Mohammed," he recited, as if we were all in class together.

I wondered where the faux designer clothes were coming from. We were only 290 miles from the Chinese border as the crow flies, so I wouldn't be surprised if they came from there. We were still on the old Silk Road after all. It didn't seem too far-fetched for the merchandise to have evolved not only from silk to heroin over the centuries, but to fake Gucci sweaters as well.

In the next village over, another group of kids came running toward me, and while I shook their little hands and exchanged names with them, I wondered why they weren't in school. Or was it the weekend? I had no clue what day of the week it was. Besides loading and unloading my stuff, editing videos, and riding, I no longer had a set routine. At least, not one that required me to know what day of the week it was.

I took my phone out of my pocket and opened the calendar. It was Saturday.

When I finally rode through the gates of the guesthouse I'd chosen in Qal'ai Khumb, exhausted by the long day, I was greeted by its young owner. He looked at me and smiled before asking in Russian: "Do you understand Russian?"

"No Russian," I admitted.

I followed him to the entrance and hesitated at the door. The last 16 miles to Qal'ai Khumb had been extremely muddy, and I had done several river crossings with Basanti. My boots were sopping wet and caked in mud. The owner turned around and bent down to take a closer look at my boots. He pursed his lips as if to say. *I guess they'll do*, and gestured to a corner where I could take them off. While I, teetering clumsily, undid the Velcro and pulled them off, I watched him from the corner of my eye put out a pair of pink slippers for me. My socks were so wet that I could've wrung them out, so I went ahead and took those off too.

"It's wet," I said apologetically, stepping into the pink slippers. It was such a ridiculous transition from motorcycle adventurer to slipper princess that I burst out laughing.

"Nice slippers." I giggled stupidly as I followed him up the stairs to my room, which was very neat with two twin beds and a rug on the floor.

A little while later I sat in the restaurant in the building next door. There I was served steamed dumplings with meat called *manti*, and a small plate of vegetables. I hadn't eaten anything since I'd had breakfast that morning in Dushanbe, and my stomach rumbled so loudly that I could hear it. I hungrily dug in, burning my tongue on the hot *manti*.

Chapter 9

The Wakhan Valley

Miles: 12,315

The next morning, I woke up on a hard mattress and felt just as hungry as I had the night before. Breakfast was served in the same small restaurant, and my face lit up when I saw the spread set in front of me. Thick, airy, freshly baked Tajik bread, tea, two slabs of butter, and two kinds of pickled fruit. I shamelessly gobbled down the bread, and to my joy the somewhat shy woman who worked there refilled my bread basket again. I tried to eat as much as I could, because I had a long day ahead of me. It was 150 miles to the village of Khorog, and I had a sneaking suspicion I would be unable again to find any food on the road today. I'd probably have to tough it out until dinner in Khorog. I was starting to get used to skipping lunch and had become an unwilling participant in the latest weight-loss trend: "intermittent fasting," which requires fasting for sixteen hours a day.

As I grabbed my boots to put them on, I winced, finding them to be soaking wet still. I sat on the bottom step of the stairs and examined them up close, as if that would magically dry them. When I turned them upside down, a pathetic trickle of water poured out of both boots. I clicked my tongue. If I had done this last night, surely they would have been dry by now. The pink loaner slippers had successfully distracted me from my own footwear. Now I'd have to ride in wet boots all day, and the thought of how cold my feet were going to be wasn't exactly encouraging. I put them on anyway and immediately felt my dry socks turn soggy.

With my duffel bag slung half over my shoulder, I sopped to my motorcycle. When all my worldly possessions were strapped down again, I pushed Basanti back a bit and got on. A small boy, probably the owner's son, stood by the fence and waved enthusiastically as I pulled away. The smile on his little face was so genuine and contagious that it made me forget all about my wet boots. I waved back as I rode through the gate and turned left.

I had 150 miles planned for today—and all 150 miles were along the Afghan border. It had rained a lot over the last few days. Even the previous night I had heard it pounding on the roof. The path had turned into a lunar landscape of deep puddles. I had figured it would take me seven or eight hours to reach Khorog, but not before long, I realized that that wasn't going to happen. At a measly fifteen miles per hour, I slogged across the muddy path beside the river Panj. Sometimes I'd try to go a little faster, but the road had so many deep potholes that I couldn't avoid them all at a higher speed. A few times, I crashed into one so hard that I worried about denting my rims. I wasn't quite sure about the kind of problems that would cause, exactly, but I'd heard so many motorcyclists say they couldn't continue on afterward, so it seemed safer to slow down a little.

The color of the Panj changed every time I dared to take my eyes off the road for a moment. Sometimes it was light gray, then at my next glance, a surreal shade of blue-green, briefly it was even turquoise and a few times I saw whitecaps. The mountains were always spectacular. I've always loved barren mountain ranges, where the different colors and structures of the rocks were on full display. Wooded mountains have their own charm, but I bored of them quickly. The path ran right below the steep cliffsides, and at some points the road was cut so close to the mountainside that it took me right underneath its cliffs and ledges.

The road conditions were generally pretty good around the villages I passed, but anywhere beyond those sections I struggled to avoid patches of loose gravel, small creeks running across the road, and gaping potholes. I made regular stops, in theory to admire the view, but in truth my body was aching so much that I had to allow my muscles short breaks. I had been so focused on the path that I'd been subconsciously riding with my shoulders all tensed up, almost squeezing the grips to a pulp. No matter how badly I tried to relax, I just couldn't.

A few miles after I'd passed the umpteenth checkpoint where I had to show my passport, I noticed a cyclist approach in the distance. It was the first time since Dushanbe that I'd seen a cyclist, and although I knew it couldn't be Valentin, I still felt a wave of joy at the thought of seeing a familiar face. The cyclist was coming from the opposite direction, and I eagerly rode toward him. Someone coming from the opposite direction always meant a valuable source of information. The guy on the bicycle looked just as happy to see me as I was to see him. We stopped and feverishly exchanged information. He was able to tell me that he'd only seen one other motorcyclist the past week, a German on a KTM, he said. Or perhaps it had been a Frenchman—he couldn't remember. How he wasn't able to distinguish a German from a Frenchman was a mystery to me, but the motorcyclist's nationality wasn't important. What really mattered was the motorcycle he was riding. "What kind of KTM was it, do you know?" I asked. "A big, heavy one or a light one?"

"No, it was a small motorcycle," he said, after giving it some thought. "It was definitely a very loud one."

"It must have been an Enduro." I nodded understandingly. Secretly, I had hoped he would say it had been a big, beefy KTM 1290 Adventure. If someone could get one of those across the Pamir, I'd probably manage on an Enfield too.

"There's still snow on the Ak–Baital Pass. I had to get off and push my bike," he warned.

My face darkened. "When were you there?"

He thought for a moment. "A week ago. No, wait, less than a week. Or was it a week?"

Apparently I wasn't the only one who had left my sense of time at the breakfast table.

"Maybe it won't be so bad once I get there," I said hopefully.

He nodded. "Maybe."

After I'd given him my information about the road from the Afghan border to Dushanbe, we shook hands and went our separate ways. Sometimes the locals were able to give me good advice or information about parts of my route, but the best intel usually came from other travelers. I could be certain their information was fresh, and that it came from someone with a similar perspective on what was safe and what wasn't. Just as the Thai had insisted that Malaysia was "So very dangerous!" while the Malaysians told me the same thing about Thailand, I was sometimes told I had to be very careful in the next big city, because it was totally unsafe compared to [enter random city here where I was now]. Fellow travelers usually gave me a more nuanced lay of the land.

–

It was already five-thirty when I finally reached Khorog. I rolled onto the driveway of the Pamir Lodge, which was a favorite among travelers just like the Green House Hostel in Dushanbe. I was hoping to meet some other people there, but apart from a small tent in the corner it was completely deserted. I looked around, disappointed, and saw a man sitting in a tiny wooden booth. Even though I couldn't see anybody else, I asked: "Do you have a room available?"

He nodded and I threw my hands up in the air triumphantly. I was exhausted after the day I'd had, but the adrenaline of riding along the border with Afghanistan all day gave me a final push. I was just closing the door to my room behind me to get something to eat when the door next to it opened. It turned out there was another traveler here after all! When I looked at him, thrilled, he smiled broadly and introduced himself as Ganesha.

"The patron saint of travelers," I responded.

"That's right," he said, laughing.

Ganesha was the name of the Hindu god of wisdom, prosperity, and luck, but he was also the protector of travelers. Contrary to the Hindu god, this Ganesha thankfully didn't have an elephant head. He was from Singapore, he told me, and was on his way to Montreal.

"To Montreal?" I repeated in surprise. "Montreal as in Canada?"

I couldn't begin to guess what a twenty-year-old Singaporean was doing at the border between Tajikistan and Afghanistan while on his way to Montreal.

Ganesha looked at me and grinned. "I've been accepted to university there." He paused, as if this snippet of information explained everything. When I didn't say anything, he continued, "I finished Singapore's two years of compulsory military service last November, so I had ten months before the new academic year started. I thought that would be enough time to reach Canada without taking a plane."

"So you got here from Singapore overland. But what will you do when you reach the Atlantic Ocean?"

"I'm not sure yet," he mused. "I think I'll try to hitch a ride on a container ship or something like that."

I was immediately fascinated by this young adventurer. He traveled by bus, train, or hitchhiking and slept in a tent or on the couches of hospitable locals. He roughly outlined his route so far, and my ears perked up when he mentioned China. I'd been to Beijing before, but never to the west of China, to the Xinjiang province.

"Xinjiang, what was that like? I thought China doesn't want anyone snooping around there?"

"Not usually, no," Ganesha agreed. He told me what he'd seen there, how Uyghurs were surrounded by Chinese soldiers at random and forced to sing the Chinese anthem. The soldiers never forced him, a Singaporean, to do the same, but he did get repeatedly interrogated and had his pocketknife confiscated at some point. With a somber look on his face, he told me how he'd used that knife almost daily to prepare his meals and how he missed it now that it was gone.

His attempt to hitchhike out of China had seemed very suspicious to the border guards, and they'd subjected him and his belongings to a thorough search. They'd turned his backpack upside down to spread its contents on the floor. Ganesha had hoped that his hard drive, carefully tucked away in his dirty laundry, wouldn't get noticed, but that failed. One of the guards fished the hard drive out of the pile of his things and connected it to their computer. Then, they proceeded to tediously check its contents, opening each and every file.

"I knew I wouldn't always have access to the internet on this trip, and that there would be strict censorship, so I had come prepared," began Ganesha. Before leaving Singapore, he had painstakingly downloaded one terabyte of spicy videos from the Web in case he needed some nighttime entertainment.

"So there I was, while those Chinese border guards clicked and watched every video. I thought I'd die from embarrassment." He added: "I came out two years ago."

He shot me a meaningful look and then burst out in such uncontrollable laughter that it made me cackle. We couldn't stop—we laughed until the tears rolled down our cheeks and my stomach started to hurt. A couple of border guards in an extremely conservative part of China systematically going through his entire collection of frisky videos to rule out the possibility that he was a spy was the most hysterical travel story I'd heard in a long time.

—

I stayed in Khorog the next day. There was rain forecasted, and I had planned a rest day. I needed to recuperate, wash my stinking, dirty motorcycle clothes, give Basanti a thorough checkup, and, most importantly, hear more of Ganesha's stories. While examining Basanti's rear wheel, I was horrified to find a small piece of metal sticking out of the tire. I instinctively pulled it out, then briefly stood there holding the sharp object. I didn't hear any air escaping from the tube, so I assumed I'd narrowly avoided a puncture. I grabbed my tire pressure gauge to make sure. The reading was the same as always, and I breathed a sigh of relief. If I'd kept going for one more day, the metal would undoubtedly have penetrated deeper into the rubber, and I *would* have gotten a puncture. I'd been so lucky to discover this now! I rarely checked my tires, something I might do daily if I were a more sensible person. I didn't allow myself the time. In the mornings, I was so eager to start riding that it never felt like I had a moment to spare for something so tedious.

My departure from Khorog the day after meant saying goodbye to Ganesha, who left to hitchhike toward Dushanbe. As we said our farewells, I pressed my Swiss army knife into his hands.

"Here, now you have a knife again."

His gaze flashed to the knife and then back to me. "Thank you," he said then, and I saw that his eyes were wet.

We embraced and wished each other a safe journey.

Upon leaving Khorog, I had to make an important decision about my route. I was at a crossroads. I could follow the M41, or the Pamir Highway, which had pretty good tarmac from here, or I could take a detour through the Wakhan Valley. The latter would mean continuing to ride south along the border with Afghanistan to reach the Wakhan Corridor. This narrow strip of territory stuck out of the northeast of Afghanistan like an outstretched finger. Because of it, Tajikistan didn't share a land border with Pakistan, and that had been exactly what the British intended when they ensured this valley became part of

Afghanistan in 1893. Afghanistan had essentially been used as a buffer between the British Empire and the Russian Empire.

Unlike the M41, the road through the Wakhan Valley was mainly unpaved, and in terrible condition. But riding alongside the gorgeous Panj river and the view over Afghanistan was far from boring. Not far from Khorog also lay the only opportunity to cross the river and ride a short distance through Afghanistan. At the time, Taliban fighters had yet to enter the region, and it was considered safe. I had already spent a good amount of time gazing longingly at the river and the road on the other side. I really wanted to see the Afghan villages up close and meet the people who lived there. But I still couldn't bring myself to cross. Contrary to what had happened in Iran, where I'd been showered with positive reactions to the videos I'd made there, my journey through Tajikistan had revealed a totally different side of the internet. I'd been receiving serious digital threats for a week now. A stranger had shared my journey on a far-right website, and the most horrible messages were coming my way. How *dare* I come here, as a white woman on my own— that was, according to them, basically asking for it.

"I'm waiting for that LiveLeak video in a couple months where you're raped for a week then beheaded."

"I'm going to laugh so hard when they find your decapitated, raped body out there in the middle of bumfuck nowhere."

"I hope you get jumped, you crazy moron."

"Just so you all know, she has been raped and killed."

And those were the friendliest ones. I'd always known there was a risk to sharing my travels on YouTube, but I never would have thought it would escalate so quickly, so horribly. Even though I knew I'd be perfectly safe riding on the opposite side of the river for a little while, I also knew it would only bring about even bigger, more hateful reactions.

The fact that there were people out there who were hoping I'd be raped and beheaded filled me with dread, and I was sleeping poorly. I wasn't afraid of the people from Tajikistan, or from Afghanistan, but I *was* afraid of a bunch of strangers on the internet. Eventually, I decided not to cross the river. It wasn't worth the consequences. Following the road through the Wakhan Valley was the closest I could get to Afghanistan without ever setting foot in the country, so that's what I did.

—

It took me two days to cross the entire valley. Sometimes it was like I pictured it: a valley, wide and accented by mountains in the distance, and other times it was so narrow that it was more gorge than valley. The river came in new colors that I hadn't seen before, including a Gatorade blue. I barely saw any other vehicles on the road. A few times I passed trucks from Soviet times, like a ZIL-131, that were now only used to transport rocks for road construction, and the occasional old Lada. Other than that, Basanti and I had the road all to ourselves. I wondered if people on the Afghan side of the border could hear Basanti's low rumble echo between the mountains. The thought brought a smile to my face— only motorcyclists can truly understand the appeal of a ridiculously loud exhaust.

For the first time since I'd started the Pamir, I saw snow piled up on the side of the road. A grim warning of what would be coming my way in the coming days.

I was riding along, tall trees lining either side of my view, when I noticed a house with a bright blue roof and a man standing by the side of the road. He gestured for me to stop and to my own surprise, I did.

"Hey," I said half questioningly.

"Narzan?" he asked. When I didn't react immediately, he leaned toward me and said it again, this time a little louder. "Narzan."

"Narzan," I repeated, still not understanding. I didn't know that "Narzan" was the Tajik version of Evian. He nodded and pointed at a nearby fence. "Mineral water," he said.

But I didn't hear him and instead asked a nonrelevant question: "Tea?"

"Tea, coffee," said the man. "Narzan," he repeated once again, and for a moment it felt like we were both just saying random words.

I decided that it wouldn't hurt to make a stop here and find out what this Narzan was all about. Besides, all that talk of beverages had made me thirsty. I parked next to an old woman standing beside the road and followed the man a few steps down to the river. When he turned around, I saw that he was holding up a small green plastic jug. He repeated again that this was Narzan—mineral water. I wasn't sure if I was meant to wash my face with it or drink it, but I went for the latter.

"Thanks," I said in Russian, before placing my lips against the plastic jug.

"Drink it, sweetheart, drink it," the woman said encouragingly, still standing next to Basanti and watching me closely. "She has a beautiful face," she added.

She spoke either Russian or Pamiri, and unfortunately her sweet words were lost on me in that moment. The man gestured that it was now time for tea, and I followed him toward the blue-roofed house. At the back of the house was a small balcony with a magnificent view over the Panj, and I sat down at the table. The man placed a cup of tea in front of me and disappeared back into the house. While I took small sips of tea and watched the river, a younger woman approached me. She wore an apron in the same bright shade of blue as the Panj behind us, and a headscarf with polka dots.

"Pirozhki? Pirozhki?" she asked.

All my brain managed to turn that into was *"Ruski, Ruski."* I thought she was asking me if I spoke Russian.

"No, I don't understand," I said in Russian. Thankfully she didn't let my random reply throw her off, and not long after she came back with a plate of piroshki and put it in front of me. I had seen these buns before, in Dushanbe, and knew that they tasted like *oliebollen*, the deep-fried dough balls we Dutch traditionally eat on New Year's Eve. I ate two before being stuffed to the gills from all their deep-fried greasiness. It took some convincing before the woman accepted my payment. At first, she didn't want to hear of it, then she only wanted to charge me for the *pirozhki*, and only after I insisted some more did she let me pay for the tea as well. I hid a tip under my plate and walked outside.

When I got back to Basanti, the old lady was still there. She wore a black leather jacket, one that rather looked like a motorcycle jacket, over a long dress. Her arms loosely crossed, she studied me as I prepared to take off.

"Goodbye," I said, so I could use my second-favorite Russian word. *Dosvidaniya.*

"Goodbye," she replied.

—

After following the river for miles, I eventually turned down a side road so I could finally get a look at the valley from a different perspective. The narrow path climbed gradually, until I finally stood on top of a mountain and looked down at the valley below. I stopped to admire the remnants of the Fortress of Yamchun from a distance. The fortress was a silent witness to the past, when it was part of a prosperous corridor along the Silk Road. It was the ruler of the Kushan dynasty who had realized that the merchants traveling down the Silk Road were in need of protection. In exchange for road tax, he offered them safe passage to transport their goods. Many fortresses were built to protect the merchants from raiders and protect the empire from neighboring clans. The Fortress of Yamchun was built around the third century B.C. and expanded further in the twelfth century. I admired the crumbling fortress for a while, and almost couldn't believe it was still standing, balancing on top of a strongly eroded hill.

But before long, my gaze was drawn beyond the fortress.

There, in the distance, emerged the peaks of the Hindu Kush, the legendary mountains that separated Afghanistan from Pakistan. Ten of the most important rivers in Asia originated there, including the Indus, the Ganges, the Mekong, and the Yangtze. I knew of the tales of Alexander the Great, who crossed them to reach India, and of Genghis Khan, who had roamed around there in his insatiable desire for conquest. The mountains felt so close, I swore I could almost touch them.

My eyes started to water because of the cold wind that blew from the snowy summits of the Hindu Kush, straight into my face. In my mind, I let myself drift along to the top of the tallest peaks of Afghanistan. So much fighting had taken place in those mountains, both in the past and the present. Right now it was so quiet that it was hard to imagine that. Other than the wind blowing around my ears, I couldn't hear anything else. No raging highway, no car horns, no airplanes, let alone explosions or the *rat-a-tat* of firearms. I couldn't have known then that it wouldn't be long before everything would change here. I sniffled, pulled my helmet back over my head, and fastened the strap.

–

I rode back down into the valley and again a cyclist was coming from the other direction. Even from a distance I could see that it wasn't a traveler, thanks to the absence of panniers. I came to a stop and so did he. While I switched off Basanti's engine, he lithely swung his leg over the frame and dismounted. It was an older man wearing a black beret, a neat blue button-down, and a long black blazer.

"Normal?" I called out in Russian while giving a questioning thumbs-up. This meant: *Everything okay?*

The man held up his hand and simultaneously threw his head back. This could mean anything from *What do you want?* and *Do you have anything to tell me?* I guessed it meant: *Where are you from?*

"*Niederlandia,*" I replied. He nodded, I'd given the correct answer. "How are you?" I asked tentatively in Russian. He gave me a thumbs-up.

"Good?"

"Good," he confirmed. "And you?"

"Good."

"How many days did it take you to come here from Ireland?" he asked.

"Five," I said, holding up a hand with the fingers splayed. The conversation was held together by misunderstandings neither of us were aware of.

He thoughtfully shook his head and I giggled quietly, the way I always giggle when I feel awkward. "Today Langar and tomorrow Alichur," I tried to explain my travel plans in Russian.

"You alone?" he asked.

I nodded. "Noraly," I introduced myself.

"Nurali," he echoed, in disbelief.

I understood his surprise. My name was Arabic in origin, and Nurali was a common name in Central Asia—for men though. I pointed at him to signal I was asking for his name.

"Kirgizbek," he said, which literally meant "Son of a Kyrgyz."

I repeated his name and held out my hand. He confidently grabbed it and we firmly shook hands. We tried to talk a little while longer, but we had exhausted my Russian vocabulary. There were no more words left.

I looked at Kirgizbek and he said: "Good."

It was time for both of us to go. We said goodbye and he carried on cycling, on his black bicycle with coaster brakes.

–

The next morning, I studied my route over a breakfast of fried eggs and warm porridge. I had made it to Langar, still on the Afghan border, and from here it was another 80 miles over an unpaved mountain road to get back to the M41, the Pamir Highway. There wouldn't be any villages along the entire stretch, and the road would no longer follow the river Panj. I stared at the six hairpin bends immediately outside of Langar, leading straight up a mountain ridge. This was a legendary portion of an already legendary route, and I knew that many travelers had been forced to turn around here because they didn't make it up the mountain.

I had rented a room for next to nothing with a family living on the outskirts of Langar. The daughter of the family, who I estimated was about twenty, spoke English incredibly well. She wore blue jeans with traditional sandals, and a yellow fringed scarf. Her long hair was tied up in a loose bun. As I was busy turning Basanti around in the small courtyard, she came outside to see me off.

The previous night, I had seized the opportunity to talk to her in English. I had so many questions about her people, their culture, and their lives, but so far the language barrier had prevented such conversations. Besides English, she also spoke Wakhi, one of the many Pamir languages related to those of East Iran. Tajik, the language that was spoken in other parts of Tajikistan, was related to the southwestern Iranian languages, just like Farsi. Some linguists even viewed the Persian languages of Tajikistan, Iran, and Afghanistan as dialects of the same language. Either way, I didn't understand a word of any of them.

We talked about Navruz, which isn't just an important holiday for Iranians, but for Pamiris too. She told me about the dishes she had made for its feast and she even showed me two instruments that were played during Navruz. She had carefully taken the *rubab*, a plucked lute with three main strings, from a wooden chest. This was a well-known musical instrument from the region and the national instrument of Afghanistan. She also showed me a *daf*, which looked like a tambourine, only without the little bells. I had tried to tempt her into playing it, but she had been shy and had only softly tapped her fingers on the *daf* a couple of times. She was a beautiful woman, and her sparkling eyes stood out against her flawless tanned skin.

"Have a good trip," she said with a laugh, pulling me back into the here and now.

"Thank you," I called back.

My mind has often wandered back to this young Pamiri, whose name I regretfully didn't know. Two years after I said goodbye to her, the Taliban gained control of the Wakhan Corridor in Afghanistan for the first time in history, during their 2021 summer offensive. As a result, Taliban fighters were roaming around on the other side of the Panj. The silence I'd felt when I looked at the Hindu Kush, out there by the fort, had been broken once again. Thousands of Afghans and hundreds of ethnic Kyrgyz fled the Wakhan Corridor, into Tajikistan, because they wanted to be able to send their kids to school—something the Taliban had instantly forbidden. I hoped that she, the children who had waved to me along the way, and all the other Pamiris I had met in the Wakhan Valley remained safe. And continued going to school.

Chapter 10

One with the Pavement

Miles: 12,615

I squeezed through the gate of the house and rode past the line of trees back to the main road. The first section after Langar was horrible, as if a ZIL-131 had dumped a full load of fresh gravel the night before. I had great difficulty keeping my bike balanced on the loose surface, but I didn't come down. As I turned onto the first corner, I knew I had begun the long ascent of hairpin bends.

The road was nothing more than a horizontal interruption of the steep rocky mountainside covered with loose rocks. My eyes were glued to the track so I wouldn't accidentally disappear over the edge and plummet back down into the valley. In first gear and with the clutch slightly disengaged, I tried to keep enough momentum so I wouldn't stall halfway through a turn. This was exactly what I'd practiced with Peter in Oman, except that now I had to do it on a heavily loaded bike with only half the power of his CCM. In my head, I counted the hairpin bends and I let out a sigh when I spotted the sixth one ahead of me. To my astonishment an old RV with Swiss license plates appeared, parked right next to the track after the last turn.

As I came closer, I noticed the hood was up—a sign that things weren't going according to plan. I pulled over and waved. A young guy in dusty black jeans with a hole in them and a worn cap on his head turned around and waved back. He was holding a bottle of water and peered back again at the engine of the old Fiat Ducato RV. It wasn't an ideal place to have engine trouble. For the life of me I couldn't understand how he'd gotten this monstrosity up the mountain in the first place.

"Trouble?"

"Not at all," he replied airily, while looking at the bottle of water. "Just a little overheating problem."

I looked gravely at the engine under the hood, as though they'd called roadside assistance, and I was the mechanic on duty today. He turned to face me, and I noticed he had a mustache and two gold earrings in his left ear.

"Do you want coffee?" he said, changing the subject to more important matters. "My girlfriend just made some, why don't you go inside." He tilted his head toward the door of the RV.

"Yes, please," I answered spontaneously. Good coffee on the Pamir was a rare thing, so I wasn't about to let this opportunity slip through my fingers. I stuck my head through the doorway of the RV and my eyes were met by his girlfriend's. She looked to be in her twenties, and she had a small piercing just above her upper lip. Her thick dark hair almost reached her belly button. She had a stunning presence.

"Hi," I said.

"Come in, come in," she said, already pulling a clean mug out of a cupboard and pouring coffee into it. They were both from the French-speaking part of Switzerland, and the ceiling cupboards inside the RV were covered with maps of Central Asia with pencil marked routes.

"I don't get how you guys made it up here through those switch-backs," I said, getting right to the point.

She slammed down the coffeepot and looked at me wide eyed. "It was so, so scary," she stammered. She relived the fear so intensely that even I could feel it in my gut. "Twice we didn't have enough momentum and rolled back, right at the cliff! We should have never, never taken this road, but well." And then she shrugged. "Can't do anything about it now. Now we just have to keep going."

She filled the mug and handed it to me. I gratefully took a few sips of the hot coffee and for a moment, we were both quiet. Neither of us knew what the road ahead of us looked like, so we talked about how the journey so far had gone. When the coffee was finished, I said goodbye and walked back to Basanti.

"See you tomorrow," the guy called after me, emptying another bottle of water under the hood. They planned to take the same route as me, and we talked about meeting again the next day. I reluctantly left them behind and spent the rest of my day wondering how they'd gotten on. Did he manage to get the RV to work again? Whenever I hit a tricky part, I was convinced that it would be impossible to do with an old RV, and wondered if they would turn around.

There was no longer any green in sight, and no trees either. The mountains were now only bare, pointy, and snowcapped. Just like in Zanskar, in India, I came across a few groundhogs with their thick coats hobbling quickly to their burrows as I approached. The road felt like I was riding on an endless ribbed sweater. I stopped and got off to inspect the corrugations up close. From the seat of my motorcycle the road appeared smooth, so I didn't get why it felt so horribly bumpy. I squatted and studied the fine gravel that stretched out before me like a washboard.

Then, I whipped my head around thinking I'd heard a car. My eyes swept the ridges of the road in the distance, all the way to where the road descended toward the valley. But there was no one in sight for as far as the eye could see. Even though I didn't see anything, I felt like I was being watched. In truth, the main reason I'd stopped had been to pee, but I suddenly changed my mind. A bitter wind was whipping my hair into my eyes and mouth, which I had to keep furiously sweeping out of my face. I pulled up the collar of my motorcycle jacket a little further. I reached over my shoulder and grabbed the hose of my backpack to drink a few mouthfuls of water. I wasn't thirsty at all, and didn't want to pressure my bladder any further, but I still made myself drink a little. Because of the high altitude, a constant ache lingered around my head like a light fog, and I didn't want to make it any worse. I straightened up the scarf I wore across my nose and mouth to fend off the cold and got my gloves back on. It had only been a few weeks ago that I was suffering from the heat in the Iranian desert, and yet I now found myself longing for that warmth.

Not much later, I arrived at a large military checkpoint—the last place with people before I had to cross the mountain pass toward the Pamir Highway. A yellowish-white barrier was lowered and blocking the path. To the left of the barrier, I saw some sort of white mini bunker that had a hole so small that logically it would only fit the barrel of a gun. A little farther down, beyond the barrier, stood a larger, white building.

"Hello?" I said, uncertain.

Silence.

"Hello?" I called out, a little louder this time.

I turned the ignition key to the right and beeped my horn twice in quick succession. I heard and saw nothing but more deathly silence. I didn't know whether the barrier was down because the guards happened to be on their lunch break or because I wasn't supposed to continue past this point at all, but there was nobody to ask. I wasn't very keen to wait in the cold for someone to finally show up, so I started Basanti again. I carefully rode toward the barrier, and as it turned out my fairing could just fit underneath. I bent forward, and with my head in the gap between the left wing mirror and the fairing, I could just squeeze through. Like an escaped prisoner, I passed underneath the barrier, my motorcycle, belongings, and self included. The barrier now behind me, I passed the larger, white house and shouted one last "Hello?" by way of formality, but nobody came out.

Even though it wasn't a very big deal, my barrier breakthrough felt like a small victory and encouraged me to cover the final stretch to the Pamir Highway. But as I kept going and saw nothing but deserted, vast mountains ahead, a suffocating feeling suddenly crept up on me. Earlier, I'd mentally designated the military checkpoint as an important point of reference; a place where I knew I could find people in case of emergency. That way, I could always know how far away I was from help, if I needed it. But despite seeing a few buildings, I wasn't sure now if there were any people around at all. Not being able to make a quick calculation of the distance to my rescue made me feel anxious. The vastness of the stark mountain scenery no longer excited me, but made me painfully aware that besides myself, there was nobody here.

I tried to keep riding at a constant pace and focus on the track. Every time I managed to get through a difficult section, like parts with slippery snow, I'd feel calm and strong, but the next moment, when I'd reached a fork in the road and was unsure whether I was still on the right path, I would wonder if this hadn't been one big mistake.

I rode like this for miles, in a mixture of delight and torture. I reached a mountain pass at 10,500 feet and the icy wind sucked all the air out of my lungs. The cold lashed out so greedily that a slippery layer of ice had formed on the small mountain lake I passed. I fantasized about a hot shower and a bed with a down comforter. I'd first put my soft pajamas on the radiator and then slip into them after my shower. I pictured myself pulling the comforter up over my ears, only my eyes and nose peeking out above it. I tried to force myself to think about something else, but without much success.

Every time the road changed from rocky to sandy and the surface felt different, my stomach dropped, afraid I had a flat tire. I'd ride on for a few feet with my heart in my throat, trying even harder to feel if there was something wrong. Had the piece of metal I had pulled out earlier punctured the tube after all? I should have just replaced the tube when I was safely at the hostel, I thought, angry with myself. Thanks to that piece of metal, there was now a tear in the tire that was so small you couldn't see it—but that I knew was there. I realized that, despite the demonstration I'd got in Karol Bagh and my flat tire in Malaysia, I most certainly couldn't patch a tire by myself, least of all here on some mountain pass in Tajikistan. Since the Swiss couple and their shabby RV, I hadn't seen anyone else and, honestly, I didn't expect to any longer. If I got a flat tire here, I would have no other choice than to park Basanti and sit down next to her on the dirt. I would have to spend the night here, at well over ten thousand feet altitude, without a tent. All I had was a satellite phone I'd bought in Oman. It had seemed like a good idea at the time, but now I wasn't so sure. Who was I going to call while sitting down next to my motorcycle? I didn't have a single phone number of a Tajik or someone who lived nearby, let alone the number of the local emergency services. It was suddenly, painfully clear to me how precarious this whole endeavor truly was. I didn't have the right gear, skills, or experience. I'd failed in all subjects.

Earlier in the day, I could still convince myself to stop and take a photo every once in a while, but I didn't stop anymore. I was afraid that if I stopped, the engine wouldn't start back up and I'd freeze to death along the side of the road. It was there, alone on my motorcycle on the Pamir, that I finally realized what it meant to truly travel alone. For years, I'd hailed myself as an experienced solo traveler. I had collected a small stack of full passports—the silent proof of my restlessness. By backpacking alone, I'd visited over forty countries in Asia, Latin America, and Africa. But now that I was alone, I finally understood that I hadn't been back then. I had taken buses, trains, boats, and planes. There had always been other passengers on board, or at least a driver. At the end of the day, I could only go where public transport went, and with it, all the other tourists. But there was no bus here, nor another soul to be seen.

I was freezing, I was scared, I was alone. But at the same time I realized: there was nowhere in the world I would rather be than right here. Despite the hardships of the cold Pamir, I had fallen instantly, completely, and head over heels in love with this part of the world. It felt like everything that had happened—my destroyed relationship, the forced sale of my house, my attempt to become a filmmaker—were all part of a bigger plan to get me here. Here, alone, on the Pamir. I wanted to stay here forever, in this wilderness, together with Basanti.

With 12.5 miles to go before I'd reach the paved road, I suddenly noticed two distinct bicycle tracks running through the sandy path. They occasionally disappeared on gravelly sections, but then they reappeared in the dust. I focused my attention on the tracks, which connected me to other cyclists, like an invisible cord pulling me along. I expected to see them behind every bend, but no matter how fresh the tracks seemed, I didn't catch up to them. "Wait for me," I said out loud. I steadfastly followed the tracks, and I was so consumed by the race to get closer to the cyclists beyond that I stopped noticing how cold I was. Suddenly the M41 appeared.

"The Pamir Highway!" I whooped. "I made it!"

I had never been so relieved to see pavement. As my wheels touched it, I realized that this wasn't just any pavement—it was brand-spanking-new, almost black, smooth asphalt.

I whizzed the final miles to Alichur at fifty miles an hour. After the excruciatingly slow pace I had kept the entire day, I now felt like I was going ridiculously fast. A few miles before I reached town, I finally saw the cyclists. I'd found them! It had to have been their tracks I had followed all along. I asked them, as I came to a halt beside them, and they confirmed they'd arrived on the same road as me. We agreed to stay in the same guesthouse so we could keep each other company. I went ahead and crossed the Gunt River via a small bridge and rode into Alichur.

I quickly managed to find the homestay where the cyclists were going, which had a few rooms for rent. It was a single-story, white building, and a few yaks were grazing on the small field next to it. The walls inside had been painted white as well, the floor was covered with brightly colored, low-pile rugs. I hauled my bag into the room and walked back outside to take the two spare tires inside too. I was so incredibly fed up with them that I had been sorely tempted to fling them into the river Panj a couple of times. Besides always dragging them around despite their being so unwieldy and heavy, the spare front tire also happened to give me an additional problem. It was big enough to fit perfectly around my left pannier, so that's where I'd been tying it all this time. But what I hadn't realized was that the tire stuck out from underneath the pannier, logically enough. Now that I'd had to brave one river after the other in Tajikistan, the tire kept hitting the water, yanking me off balance. The left side of the bike faced more resistance in the water than the right side, making me waltz sideways through rivers like a dressage horse.

I chatted for a while with the cyclists, who turned out to be Spanish, but soon noticed that I was too tired to hold a decent conversation. I retreated to my room and got ready to go to bed. Right when I crawled under the blanket, I realized that after all the cups of weak tea the Pamiris had given me, I needed to go to the bathroom. In Tajikistan, the toilet, a simple hole in the ground, was commonly a short distance away from the residence.

I had made it a habit not to go outside in the dark, but I had no choice. When I stepped outside, the cold hit my throat and I tightened my scarf another turn around my neck. I took a few steps toward the outhouse and suddenly froze in place, blown away by the night sky. The stars twinkled so brightly and intensely, as though they were trying to cover the Pamir with a shimmering diamond blanket. I looked up, my head tilted so far back that the back of my head touched my shoulder blades, my mouth wide open. The only time I'd ever seen a night sky like this before was in the Australian outback.

For a moment, it felt like Dave Russell was standing next to me again. Together, we had spent weeks trekking through the vast outback of Queensland, in northeast Australia. We slept in *swags*, a kind of bedroll that combined a sleeping bag and mat, looking for gold. It was my first job as an exploration geologist. It had never been my plan to become a gold digger, but somehow I became one.

The plan had originally been for me to get my PhD after I'd finished my master's research. I'd written my master's thesis on climate change. In the couple of months I spent before graduating from the organic geochemistry department in Bristol, England, I discovered the molecule isorenieratene in a laboratory. You know—*isorenieratene*. In fact, I didn't find it just once, but in rock samples from all over the world. Those rocks had been sent to me by other geologists, or I'd collected them myself. I sweet-talked my way into oil companies that had long rock cores in their archives that I could take samples from for my research. Isorenieratene is only produced by certain green sulfur bacteria that can live in anoxic conditions (without oxygen) in the top layer of the ocean. Long story, but what it came down to was that this was (more) proof that there have been moments in the history of our planet where all large oceans were without oxygen. And that— besides some green sulfur bacteria—there was basically no life possible in the oceans during those times. I had been offered a PhD position at the University of Utrecht to spend four years unraveling this matter further. I had already collected the rock samples, but I wanted to travel for a couple of months before I started my research.

That was the trip when I visited India for the first time and decided that a career in academics wasn't what I wanted after all. Instead, I backpacked through India and Southeast Asia until I was left with a meager one hundred euros in my bank account. I spent eighty of those euros on a plane ticket from Indonesia to Australia. I knew there was good money to be made in Australia, so I flew to Perth with only twenty euros left. I had never been that broke in my life. In the ridiculously expensive Perth, twenty euros wasn't even enough to pay for my first night in a hostel. Thankfully, the receptionist agreed to my promise that I'd pay at check out. I had landed in the city at 4 a.m., and after I'd thrown my bag on the bunk bed in the hostel, I immediately sprang into action. I spent a couple of dollars on printing a stack of CVs at an internet café, then walked around the city all day handing them out at dozens of cafés and restaurants. It worked. I could start as a waitress at a coffee place the next day, and I stayed there for a few weeks.

Eventually, it dawned on me that Perth was the mining capital of Australia, and geologists were in high demand everywhere. I applied and immediately landed a job at Breakaway Resources, as an exploration geologist. The offer came as a huge surprise to me, because I had applied for the position of field assistant—the same position as Dave Russell. The president of Breakaway Resources at the time, David Hutton, had looked at my master's degree in geosciences and said: "Field assistant? But you have a geoscience degree. You can go ahead and start as a geo." I had simply nodded, dumbfounded.

During my first few months as a field geologist, I had no idea what I was supposed to do or what was going on. You see, I had graduated in organic geochemistry, which was a pretty far cry from exploration geology, or knowing where and how to find nickel, copper, or gold. I hadn't even gotten a bachelor's degree in geology but had progressed from my undergrad degree in biology. If I told you I was suffering from impostor syndrome, I'd be lying. I personified impostor syndrome. Ultimately, it was Dave Russell who taught me everything, even though he didn't have a geology degree himself, and I was technically his superior. Admittedly, Wikipedia helped too, teaching me in the late hours of the night what massive sulfides were and what they had to do with finding nickel.

Dave looked like the stereotypical image I always had of Australians: his everyday uniform was a two-piece khaki outfit, the shorts just a little too short. Precisely what Steve Irwin used to wear. I adored his company. He was somewhere in his mid-fifties and had worked in the field for longer than I'd been alive. From him, I learned how to look for minerals, cook sweet potatoes in a field oven, drive a 4x4, and navigate terrain in the dark.

While he was busy with the sweet potatoes, he would point at the imposing night sky and teach me which stars formed the Southern Cross. In that remote part of Australia, I saw the Milky Way for the first time in my life, and it was so intensely beautiful that it brought tears to my eyes. Only then did I learn that the brightest "star" in the sky is actually a planet (Venus), and that the moon rises every day about fifty minutes later than the day before. As I looked at the starry night sky from the highlands of Tajikistan, I wondered if at that same moment, Dave was outside too, looking at the stars.

Despite my imposter syndrome and only tangentially relevant degree, I had still been successful in Australia. I found gold, copper, nickel, silver, lead, and zinc. David Hutton was so happy with me that when my contract ended, he offered me another job, including a promotion. Who would have thought—I certainly hadn't.

–

The next day, I was woken up early by the smell of breakfast. I wasn't sure if it was the smell of the *kush*, a type of warm porridge, or the dried yak poop it was cooked over. I was lying on a thin floor mattress, and the chill of the concrete floor underneath had seeped into my back. In an attempt to fall asleep on the thin mattress, I had tried every position. In the end, on my stomach was most comfortable, but I'd kept waking up because the pillow stank and my entire face was pressed into it from that position.

After devouring a plate of *kush* and knocking back two cups of weak tea, I began loading up my stuff. I looked at Basanti and had to admit that she looked horrible. Besides all the mud and dirt, the way she'd been packed was quite frankly beyond ridiculous. With the spare rear tire tied half over the top box and duffel bag, my things towered over the motorcycle like the Hindu Kush over the Wakhan Valley. It was a miracle that she didn't instantly tip backward with the unequal distribution of weight.

I peered into the distance for a while and wondered if the Swiss couple in the old RV had made it to Alichur too. It frustrated me that I didn't know what had happened to them. I urged the Spaniards to keep an eye out for an old RV with a young Swiss couple, though I wasn't sure what I was trying to achieve with that. Even if they did, there was no way they'd be catching up to me on their bicycles to tell me about it.

My plan for today involved two simple steps: ride to Karakul, my last stop in Tajikistan, and track down some gas. Step two especially had me on edge. I hadn't seen a gas station since Dushanbe, and I had been sent packing twice from places that were supposed to have fuel. *All out*, was their clear message. I had already emptied my jerrycans, with a gallon of gas each, into my main tank, but I suspected I wouldn't make it all the way to Kyrgyzstan on that. My only chance to find gas was in the town of Murghab, which also happened to be the highest town in Tajikistan, sitting at an altitude of 11,975 feet.

I set course for Murghab on the M41. It was as if all color had stayed behind in the Wakhan Valley, leaving only a selection of browns and grays to choose from here. I saw small herds of yak and sheep wandering the brown fields with not a green sprout in sight. What they survived on was a complete mystery to me. That morning, I didn't see a single vehicle or person. It was the Pamir and me. The road was straight and endless and I craned my neck for a turn that never came. I studied the mountains around me. They didn't seem all that tall and impressive, but that was just an illusion from my position on the plateau. These peaks all towered high above the Alps, and yet they looked like mere hills.

I reached Murghab a few hours later. The town looked gray and bleak from a distance, as well as from up close. Life was extraordinarily tough out here, and most people barely lived to see sixty. The high altitude, the infertile land, the scarcity of water, and the extreme cold ensured that only the most determined of souls could survive here. Just outside town were three small buildings that I'd marked on my phone as the most likely place to find gas. Just before I came to a stop, a woman stepped outside.

"Hello," I said. She greeted me back. "Gas?"

"How much do you need?" she asked.

In reality, I didn't understand what she said, but that seemed like the most relevant question to me. So, by way of reply I held up both my hands, spreading my fingers.

"Ten liters, yes," she said, and immediately headed toward the smaller building.

She opened the gray metal doors and I tried to peek inside from Basanti's seat. It was pitch black in there, but I could make out the contours of a bunch of large plastic containers. As it turned out, fire safety wasn't something to concern oneself with here. She came out with a large cylindrical funnel and one of those big gallon water jugs, only now it was filled with gas. The liquid inside had a brownish-orange glow, but I didn't know if that was because of the filthy plastic container or additives to the fuel. Perhaps it was supposed to look like that? I asked her to only fill my two backup jerrycans, so I wouldn't have this dubious substance in the main tank right away. Part of me still hoped I'd make it to Sary-Tash in Kyrgyzstan with what was left in there now, and then I might not have to use this gas at all. I paid her and rode a lap through Murghab, looking for a restaurant.

The majority of Murghab's population were in fact ethnic Kyrgyz, a nomadic people. When Tajikistan became a part of the Soviet Republic in 1929, remote villages like these weren't part of the equation. That's how Murghab ended up included in the Republic of Tajikistan, even though it was mostly ethnic Kyrgyz that lived here. I turned onto a small side street and unintentionally ended up right on the *bazaar*, Murghab's shopping street. The stores were old shipping containers that had been stacked next to one another in an almost-straight line. Some containers were closed, but others had opened their doors wide. I parked Basanti next to one of the containers and strolled through the street for a bit. I needed toothpaste and soap. The shopkeepers gave me hopeful looks, but almost every shipping container was jam-packed to the ceiling with plastic junk from China. "Made in China" were the only words I could read.

The Kulma Pass, deep in the Pamir mountains, connected Murghab with China and was only 50 miles away from Murghab. Not long after the Soviet Union collapsed and Tajikistan gained its independence, the border with China reopened and a wave of Chinese goods started pouring in. This had to be where all of the knockoff Gucci sweaters were coming from. I managed to find a tube of toothpaste and bought a pair of thin mitts to wear as an extra layer underneath my motorcycle gloves, but soap curiously proved to be an impossible mission. Although I was sure soap was somewhere to be found, I couldn't be bothered with the long search. Instead, I walked back to my bike and resumed my hunt for a restaurant.

After finishing up a plate of *laghman* for the umpteenth time on this trip and lingering to stay in the cozy heat of the restaurant a little longer, I got ready to leave Murghab. Even though there was a hotel down here, and earlier in the day I had considered staying around for a night, I wanted nothing more than to leave. My desire to escape the bleakness of Murghab, suddenly longing for sunshine, won out. In my eagerness to leave, I opened Basanti's throttle just a little more than I usually did.

I was almost out of town, going at about thirty miles an hour when I suddenly spotted three goats from the corner of my eye. In a blind panic they came storming toward me at full speed, and before I knew it, they ran across the road right in front of me. I had nowhere to go, and although I squeezed my front brake as hard as I could, I couldn't avoid slamming into goat number two with my front wheel. I hit it right on the head. *I'm going to crash*, I thought. The aftermath of the collision prematurely flashed through my mind. I would come down and roll three times, wrecking Basanti and ending my adventure.

But to my astonishment, that wasn't at all what happened. The goat's head got hit so hard that it swung aside, and for my part, I just came to a stop without crashing. I jerked my head back and saw the goat lying motionless on the road. I looked ahead again, and only then noticed the soldier who was standing by the side of the road and had seen everything. I looked at him, wide-eyed and bewildered, and he immediately started gesturing frantically with his arms.

"Go, go, go!" he shouted, a worried look in his eyes.

"Okay, okay, okay," I replied and I got the hell out of there. I was convinced that I'd have to pay the goat's owner if the goat was dead, and didn't get why the soldier had gone into such a panic. Either way, I was too afraid to turn around and ask him. What if an angry mob of villagers came after me? For the next hour I pondered a reason why the soldier had sent me away so quickly.

It wasn't until I came closer to the Ak-Baital Pass that I stopped thinking about the goat. I'd become totally consumed instead by my own hands. The motorcycle gloves I'd been gifted in Dubai were summer gloves—and came with dozens of small holes for ventilation. Wonderful for Dubai's desert climate, but entirely unsuitable for winter climates on the Pamir. The icy wind cut through my skin like a thousand tiny razor blades. My hands grew so cold that at first they started aching, and then went totally numb. I tucked away my left hand as far as possible between my seat and my thigh. As long as I didn't have to change gears, I wouldn't need it anyway. My right hand had to stay gripped on the throttle to keep the motorcycle upright. The cold had also gnawed its way through my black motorcycle jacket; the warmest piece of clothing I owned. I'd never ridden at temperatures like these before and didn't have the right gear for it. Why didn't I bring any thermal underwear with me? Or something like winter gloves? I was out of my mind. Bathing in the heat of Dubai, I couldn't have imagined it to be this cold here. By the time I realized that spring was still far from arriving, I was already too far along the Pamir to find something like a motorcycle store and buy proper gear.

Luckily I was no longer suffering from headaches or other symptoms of altitude sickness, but breathing remained a challenge. At this altitude, the atmospheric pressure and oxygen concentration were sixty percent lower than at sea level, and even though my motorcycle was doing most of the work, I still caught myself panting. I climbed to the top of the pass, at 15,272 feet, and was relieved to find a snow-free road. For days I'd been dreading this pass and expecting tons of snow. The pleasant surprise of it being easier than expected here gave me a boost in courage.

I had just passed the biggest obstacle. According to my math, I only had an hour's ride left to Karakul.

But I had barely left the pass when the road suddenly turned into an unpaved mess. The corrugations in the sandy gravel were so deep and tall that I almost bounced off Basanti. I slowed down and tried to ride over them as carefully as I could. When that didn't work, I tried it again at a higher speed, but that was even worse. I pounded and stomped, hobbled and sloshed over the road, like an egg dancing up and down in a pot of boiling water. Part of me half expected the rear suspension of my bike to burst apart in an explosion of oil.

My motorcycle held up, but every hit reverberated into my spine, and I couldn't cope with the bumps sitting down. I tried to stand on the foot pegs to relieve the strain on my back, but the shocks of the washboard road made my boots slip, slamming me back down onto the seat over and over again. I sat back down and slowed down. Dazed, I looked at the road. Whose bright idea had it been to build this torturous pass?

"I want to go home. I want to go home," I kept repeating out loud. As if saying this out loud would magically get me my house back.

Suddenly, as it had at various points throughout my journey, the realization hit me that I was longing for a home that no longer existed. But this time, that yearning, for a house that no longer belonged to me, soon gave way to immense rage. I became furious with myself. After all this time, and after having traveled thousands of miles, I was still the same inadequate motorcyclist I had been when I came down the Rohtang Pass in India months ago. I still couldn't get the hang of it, was unprepared for the elements my journey would throw at me, had no clue how to navigate rough terrain like this. Even my time with Peter in Oman hadn't prepared me for this: miles of deep, bumpy tracks at more than fifteen thousand feet altitude in the biting, freezing cold. I glanced at my phone screen for the hundredth time, hoping a town would appear.

"I made it all the way here, so I have to keep going," I tried to give myself a pep talk. As long as I kept my throttle open, Basanti would bravely plod along, even if that meant she would gradually lose every screw that held her together thanks to the violent shakes and vibrations. With my half-frozen hands, I barely managed to hold on to the handlebars. The worn steering head bearings made it next to impossible to keep the motorcycle under control.

I could feel pesky tears trying to make an escape and clenched my jaws to keep them in check. My eyes stayed dry, but my jaw muscles inspired the rest of my body, and my entire posture grew rigid and tense. It wasn't any help in absorbing the hits, and it wasn't long before pain shot through my back and neck toward my head.

Then, in the distance, I saw a truck that was slowly crawling toward me. A shriek of joy escaped me. It felt like salvation was near and my struggle was going to end. I wasn't quite sure myself what I expected this truck to do for me, but the sight of another vehicle that would have people in it gave me so much strength that I kept riding. When I was some sixty feet away from them, I promptly stopped Basanti in the middle of the road and hobbled to the passenger side of the truck, which had stopped too. The door swung open before I'd even reached it and without any hesitation I clambered up the two steps and swiveled myself inside. I yanked the door closed behind me. Two Pamiris dressed in thick winter coats and fur hats stared at me, their eyes big with surprise. It must have looked pretty comical—a blond woman with a red nose and blue lips from the cold tottering off her overloaded motorcycle and unceremoniously climbing into their cabin. Without saying anything, I peeled the perforated gloves from my hands and showed my white fingers.

"Cold, I'm so cold," I muttered. I didn't bother trying to say something in Russian and simply spoke Dutch to them. The two men looked at each other and then back at me.

"*Adin kilometer,*" said the man sitting next to me. One kilometer. "House."

"House?" I repeated in English. They both nodded. I blew on my hands for a brief second, breathed in the warmth of the cabin, and nodded too.

"Thanks," I remembered to say before climbing out again, back into the cold. The truck stayed put for a little longer, until I had my helmet back on my head and my gloves on. Then its engine fired, it slowly came into motion and honked. I raised my hand and started Basanti as well. One kilometer. Just one kilometer to go.

I carried on with nothing but my fear and my determination. The men had been right: half a mile later, a house appeared. When I rode onto the property, a dog began to bark. Soon enough the front door swung open and a woman came outside. I guessed she was about my age. She looked at me in surprise and for a moment, I didn't know what to say. I couldn't explain to her what I was doing here because I wasn't quite sure myself. Thankfully, my disheveled and partially frozen appearance spoke for itself, and she beckoned me inside.

When I stepped inside, a wave of warmth washed over me. The woodstove was burning, and it was wonderfully snug. Because I'd lost all feeling in my fingers, I wrestled to get out of my dirty boots. The woman waited patiently until I had placed them in the hallway next to the door and then turned toward the living room. She pointed at the spot on the floor next to the woodstove and I gratefully sat down. Their rug was delightfully soft and I tried to sit cross-legged, but my legs were so stiff that I ended up just stretching them out in front of me.

While the woman disappeared out of the room, I took the time to take in my surroundings. A small pile of *teresken*, a kind of local juniper bush that grew in the Pamir and was used as firewood, was placed next to the stove. The room was mostly empty, apart from a wooden cabinet in the corner. The floor was covered with rugs and a number of cushions. The moment I turned around to examine the part of the room behind me, the woman entered the living room again. In her hands she held a steaming cup of tea and a small plate with a couple of warm piroshki. At this point, I would have welcomed a plate of warm spider heads, I just longed for anything warm to eat. She placed it down for me and sat down on the opposite cushion. She silently watched as I devoured the piroshki. In between bites, I desperately tried to explain to her what was going on. That I was so cold that my bones hurt. That I was all alone and afraid I wouldn't make it. That I would suffer from hypothermia before reaching Karakul and wouldn't be found until I'd turned into an icicle.

She smiled at me as I tried to tell her my story, gesturing wildly and using the few Russian words I knew. Then the door opened and a man, I assumed he was her husband, stepped inside. Pleasantly surprised, he looked at me and back to his wife. She spoke a few words I didn't understand, and then he looked at me with just as much kindness as his wife had done that entire time.

"Karakul?" he asked.

I nodded. Using my hands I mimed an undulating movement followed by a level movement. "Kilometer?"

He thought for a moment and then said: *"Pyat kilometroy,"* while mimicking the undulating movement. I knew that meant 5 kilometers—3 miles. Then he mimed a flat line with his hands. "Karakul."

I nodded understandingly. It would be 3 more miles of misery, and then the road would be paved again until Karakul. Knowing how far it would be until the road got better gave me new hope. Three miles was doable, I could handle three miles.

"Thank you," I said. I held my hands together and locked eyes with both of them for a moment. "Thank you," I repeated once more. They nodded as if what they'd done for me was no big deal. I stood up, warmed by the wood fire and with a stomach full of piroshki and tea. They led the way out of the room, and when they weren't looking, I quickly left two notes of one hundred somoni—known simply as "som" by most locals—on the rug. I knew they wouldn't want to take my money because hospitality was a given on the old Silk Road. But I couldn't just accept their generosity without giving something back.

The dog barked again when I rode off the property with renewed energy. I raised my arm high into the air and waved. I set my sights forward and embarked on the 3 remaining miles of unpaved road. I looked the Pamir right in the eye, until the Pamir was the one to look away. I don't know if it was the piroshki or simply the encouragement I'd received from the truck drivers and the young couple, but the 3 miles flew by. All of a sudden I felt a hard surface beneath my wheels again, and I wasn't getting knocked around anymore. I breathed in deeply, sucking the cold air into my lungs. I had reached Lake Karakul, a gigantic mountain lake at 11,810 feet in altitude that was surrounded by orange-colored clumps of grass. In the distance, I saw three dust devils spinning up mini-tornadoes of dirt. I had never laid eyes on such marvelous natural phenomena. I was in the high mountains and the desert at the same time.

Suddenly my dry, chapped lips cracked open and I could no longer suppress a laugh. Just look where I am! Thousands of feet in the air, in a desert with orange grass and dust devils, blue fingers and toes but life glowing on my cheeks. I blinked against the cold and two tears drew straight lines down my face.

When I finally arrived in the small village of Karakul, I didn't have to search for a place to spend the night. A man standing on the street beckoned me as soon as he saw me, and I was so exhausted that I simply followed him like a little lamb. He wore a black hat, a black body warmer over a thick sweater, and yellow work gloves. His face was tanned by the sun and he had piercing, sparkly eyes.

I parked Basanti, and when I turned around I initially thought he'd followed me. The man standing before me looked exactly like him, including the yellow work gloves, but out of nowhere, the body warmer was suddenly blue. Unless he'd swapped into different clothes in a matter of seconds, I figured he had to be a different person. Blue body warmer spoke to me energetically and he had a lithe, quick gait. While he was busy explaining that they could feed me and that I could spend the night here for one hundred som, I just wondered how on earth they could live here. So high up in the mountains, so remote, so cold, and above all, without any comfort.

In the past week, I had developed a deep admiration for the Tajiks, with their robust demeanor, resilience, and tenacity. The young man in the blue body warmer embodied all those qualities in a single human being. I followed him into the warm house and was so exhausted that all I managed to do was take off my motorcycle boots. I never left the house that day. My hair felt like straw, first dried by the heat of Iran and then split by the cold of Tajikistan. My hands were dry and weathered and my nose and mouth were so red-raw that they looked like I'd been scraping my face over the pavement for a good amount of time. I didn't look robust at all; I looked haggard.

Chapter 11

No-Man's-Land

Miles: 12,800

I woke up at the break of dawn and my body felt like I'd crashed into that truck at full speed the day before, rather than having warmed up in its cab. The fire was out and the house felt cold. I was covered by such a big pile of blankets that the weight of it was uncomfortable. Curled up underneath them, I watched the small clouds that appeared whenever I breathed out. I reached for my phone, which I'd put next to my pillow, and looked at the time. It was a few minutes after seven. I also noticed I didn't have any reception. I hadn't been able to make phone calls or access the internet since Khorog. Part of me kind of liked it—it was nice and quiet without a phone that pinged, vibrated, and presented messages.

After mustering up the courage for a while, I pushed the blankets off me and gently rubbed my stiff legs and painful shoulders. I leaned over the blankets so I could only just reach my bag and pull it toward me. I had decided to wear all my clothes layered item after item on top of each other. I didn't have that many articles with me, so I thought I should be able to manage. I was determined to arm myself better against the cold than I had the day before. Breakfast was warm rice porridge and freshly baked, soft bread. When I emptied my plate a little bit too fast, I was given another large ladleful of porridge, which rapidly disappeared too. I put my motorcycle jacket on and stepped outside. With a full, warm belly, I looked at the sky. It was crisp and pure. A cloudless blue sky stretched out before me and there was a bright sun. The cold was less fierce than I had expected and I felt optimistic about my last portion of Pamir. I was now only 31 miles away from the border with Kyrgyzstan and that meant this would be my last day in Tajikistan. *I did it*, I thought

161

proudly. I've completed the Pamir and on top of that, even crossed the Wakhan Valley. I conveniently forgot how incredibly difficult and cold it had been the past few days. With the sun on my face and the border with Kyrgyzstan within reach, it suddenly felt like it had all been a piece of cake. Turns out, I concluded, I was a pretty badass Pamir adventurer.

–

I hadn't yet left and I was already regretting my layering strategy. Protected from the wind and facing the sun, I immediately started to sweat, and my back was drenched before I even rode off. The young man in the blue body warmer, his wife and their young child, in whose house I had slept that night, saw me off.

"Goodbye," I said in Russian as they waved. I kicked Basanti into the next gear and left Karakul, turning back onto the dreadful Pamir Highway. I rode the last section of the plains, dotted with a herd of yaks grazing in the distance, when snow-topped mountains emerged dead ahead. The view was a masterpiece, and I couldn't suppress a smile.

The border with Kyrgyzstan was on top of those mountains, on the Kyzyl-Art Pass. It wasn't long before I noticed the road was starting to climb. The asphalt ended and the road continued unpaved. Soon, I was crossing small frozen streams of water. I could hear the ice crack as my tires broke through. The thin gloves I'd bought on the Chinese market in Murghab and that I used as extra layer under my motorcycle gloves again didn't help much. My hands were soon hurting just as badly as they had the day before, and then they went numb again. I didn't understand how it could be this sunny while it was so terribly cold at the same time.

I realized that, yet again, I had made a terrible mistake. I couldn't quite understand: Why was I so unteachable? Was it just a matter of my over-optimism? I had once again allowed myself to be thrown off by focusing only on travel distance. Thirty miles hadn't seemed like much. Usually I could cover that kind of distance in thirty minutes. But here, on an unpaved Pamir, a road covered in rocks and snow, I barely moved at ten miles an hour. At this pace, I would have to brave the cold for two and a half hours. The icy wind made my breath stick awkwardly in my throat. Even though I had already mastered the even higher Ak-Baital Pass, I once again struggled with a lack of oxygen. I gasped and panted for breath that never came. My teeth were chattering so hard that it wouldn't have surprised me if the guards at the border could hear me coming already. My numbness had made it so hard to keep the throttle open that I involuntarily closed it every now and then, only to reopen it all the way with a jerk. From a distance, it must have looked like it was my first time on a motorcycle. Suddenly I no longer felt like the badass Pamir adventurer of that morning.

Eventually I reached the border, chilled to the bone. This was the border post of Tajikistan, and I saw a collection of small, white buildings. I stopped Basanti in front of the lowered barrier, right next to a car with luggage piled high on its roof. I awkwardly hopped on my left foot as I pulled my right leg over the seat and got off. I was completely out of breath. Like any other border crossing, some guy approached me and led me to one of the buildings. I stepped inside and was greeted by a border guard. He was wearing blue camo pants, army boots, and a short-sleeved T-shirt. A short-sleeved T-shirt!

"Cold?" he asked in English. My hands and feet hurt so much that all I could do was grunt, but because I could barely breathe, I wasn't able to say anything at all. "Your shoes," he said, pointing at them. He wasn't too stoked about my muddy motorcycle boots in his office. My frenzied gaze went to my boots and back to him, and he knew enough.

"Go on, go on," he said, having switched to Russian. *Davai davai.* He pointed at a small wooden bench for me to sit on. There was no way my numb hands would be able to take off my gloves, let alone my boots. While I tried to catch my breath and stop panting, the border guard carefully pulled off my double layer of gloves and then my boots. I carefully peeled my socks off the frozen stumps that only this morning had still been feet. There was a woodstove in the corner of the office, and the border guard placed my boots as close to it as possible.

Next, he focused his attention on my blood-drained hands. He said something to his colleague, who had joined us in the office, and shot another concerned look at my numb fingers. He briefly disappeared outside and returned with a bowl of lukewarm water. He gestured for me to put my fingers in it and said: *"Frost."* Was he worried about frostbite? I always thought your fingers had to be black to be talking about frostbite, but I trusted the Tajik's knowledge more than my own. While I laid my fingers in the bowl of lukewarm water, another man placed a tall glass of steaming tea in front of me and an extra pair of socks on the bench next to me. Delighted, I looked at the thick woolen socks. They were brand-new. He mumbled something and I thanked him three times or more. For an hour that's how I sat there—with my feet next to the woodstove, drinking hot tea, and slowly feeling my body temperature get back to normal. I was at a loss for words at the kindness of these people. When I'd warmed up enough to carry on, I put on my new woolen socks and stepped back into my boots. The border guard with the blue camo pants stamped my passport and collected Basanti's temporary import papers. I was free to leave Tajikistan.

"Eighteen kilometers to go to the border with Kyrgyzstan," I muttered as I walked toward Basanti.

This was by far the longest stretch of no-man's-land I had ever seen. The border posts of two countries were usually right next to each other, but now I had been stamped out of Tajikistan and still had to cover another 11 miles before I'd be stamped into Kyrgyzstan. I climbed onto Basanti, and at least she didn't seem fazed by the cold or altitude, because she started immediately. The barrier was held open by a man in civilian clothes, who casually stood with his hand on his hip. He was wearing sweatpants and a hoodie, but no gloves. He stood there like it was the dead of summer, even as it had only taken a few minutes outside for me to feel again like a walking ice sculpture.

I rode past him but didn't get very far. Less than thirty feet later, still on the Tajik side of the border, my rear tire got stuck in the mud. It seemed like the snow had only just melted, and what was left behind were deep tracks through sticky mud. I pushed and pulled at the handlebar in an attempt to free my rear wheel, but I only dug myself in deeper. Another border guard, one I hadn't seen before, came toward me and pointed out the best muddy rut to ride through. Then he gave Basanti a big push and I was free. I slogged on for a while, passed a final passport checkpoint, and was then truly free to leave Tajikistan.

The last barrier opened up before me and I rode in between two large, cylindrical buildings with windows on all sides. I wondered if they were some kind of holding cell. I didn't have much time to ponder how they'd gotten these two monstrosities up the mountain and what exactly they were used for. With the Tajik border post now behind me, snowy mountains appeared before me and the road immediately turned bad again. It was a deep, slippery muck, and the wind started to pick up. The icy gusts blew so hard that drifts of snow swept across the mud.

I wasn't going very fast to begin with; now it seemed like the wind would blow me in the opposite direction, straight back into Tajikistan.

I carefully tried to pick my way through the strips of ice, slippery mud, and tufts of snow. A few times my front wheel slid out from under me and I almost lost control of the bike. My only thought was: *Don't fall down. Don't fall down. Don't fall down.* I had already dropped Basanti dozens of times since I'd left India and picked her back up dozens of times too. But I was panting just as hard again as when I arrived at the Tajik border post, and I knew there was no way I'd be able to lift my 440-pound companion in a state like this. If I came down, I would be stuck in no-man's-land, without any help likely to pass by anytime soon.

I was on my own, and I was exhausted. It was the altitude I had been at for quite a while now, but it felt like more so because I was pushing my physical and mental limits day in and day out. I was living in a constant state of excitement and fear. My emotions rose and fell, just like the peaks and valleys around me. Everything I did was so far away from what I knew and was familiar with that nothing felt safe or secure. I had no faith in my own skills or knowledge, was left to hold on only to my hope of a good ending.

While I feverishly counted down the miles to Kyrgyzstan's border post, I was taken aback by the spectacular mountains I was riding through. I was convinced that there was no place in the world as beautiful as the Pamir. It was the vastness of the endless mountaintops, near and far, that both inspired fear and filled me with a profound sense of freedom. I felt utterly alive in a way I never had before. Apparently, I had to fear losing my life before I could reach this state of being.

I finally understood what mountaineers might have experienced as they climbed dangerous summits. The pain, the risk, the fear, and the fight are as much part of the climb as the height itself. No matter how scared I had been, I could hardly believe it was all real. That I was truly riding my motorcycle, alone, through the most breathtaking stretch of no-man's-land I had ever seen. If nobody else wanted it, I'd take it. It was all mine.

Don't fall. Don't fall. Don't fall. I was so consumed by this mantra that I no longer felt the pain in my fingers and toes. The path ran steadily from the mountain pass toward the valley until suddenly, the road was paved. I was so incredibly relieved when I felt the calm, safe asphalt under Basanti's wheels that I wanted to cling onto the feeling and never let go. For the time being, I had been cured of my urge to brave unpaved roads. Pavement was wonderful!

I had yet to even reach Kyrgyzstan's border, and I was already convincing myself that there was nothing much to see in that country, and that I might as well stick to the delightful asphalt all the way to Almaty, in Kazakhstan. I stopped in Sary-Tash, the first village on the Kyrgyz side, found a room in the first guesthouse I saw, and flopped down onto the bed. As the heater roared at full blast and I wasn't cold for the first time in days, it dawned on me: I had completed the Pamir. I was overcome by such a sense of bliss that I wondered if this was what people felt when they used drugs. I was on a Pamir high, and it was amazing.

High or not, I looked like a large bag of flour had been dumped over me. I showered for the first time in a week, thoroughly scrubbing away the sweat, dirt, and a whole host of mortal fears. The water was cold, and it pained and caressed my skin at the same time. The Pamir had kicked me down a three-story staircase, or at least, that's how I looked and felt.

For two days, all I did was eat and sleep. I stuffed myself with *beshbarmak*, Kyrgyzstan's national dish, made of stewed lamb's meat and flat noodles. I couldn't bear the sight of *laghman* or *plov*, so I ate dumplings and *shashlik*—grilled meat skewers. I was determined to stick to paved roads for the foreseeable future and eventually left for Osh. I was technically still on the Pamir Highway, but because it was nice, smooth asphalt from that point on, I felt like it didn't really count. In Murghab I had seen China's influence in the shipping containers full of cheap junk, and here it came shaped like brand-new roads: China's "New Silk Road" project.

"Please proceed to the highlighted route," my navigation system spoke to me in a crisp British accent. I had typed in "Osh" as my destination, and it was only 112 miles. Osh sat at a measly 3,280 feet altitude, so I had left the high mountains behind now. All morning, I thought about the motorcycle parts I had ordered in Dushanbe that should have arrived in Almaty by now. Every corner reminded me that I would soon be riding with new steering head bearings, and how Basanti would finally be manageable again. I alternately rode past tall mountain peaks and boundless valleys. Every time I saw a herd of horses on the road, I stopped to admire them.

Kyrgyzstan is known for its rich horse culture and for centuries, the Kyrgyz people relied on horses for transportation, herding cattle, and as currency in traditional dowries. The horses they rode were gorgeous, sturdy animals, and they looked just as resilient as the people who rode them. Most of the horses were light or dark brown, but I'd also see the occasional sand-colored one. I found them magnificent.

"Salaam," I said, greeting two shepherds on their horses. I knew they spoke Kyrgyz, a Turkish language with a Cyrillic alphabet of which I didn't speak a word. Russian was an official language as well, but for greetings the Kyrgyz used the Arabic word *salaam* since most of the locals were Muslim. Both shepherds wore a traditional, cone-shaped hat made of white felt called an *ak-kalpak*. Their lips moved and I could see that they were shouting something, but I couldn't hear anything over the bleating of their sheep. Sometimes it seemed as though Kyrgyzstan was still exclusively populated by nomadic shepherds, that's how many gigantic herds of sheep I came across. The shepherds were unfazed by the fact that this was supposed to be a highway, and they took their sweet time sauntering across the road on their horses, herding hundreds of sheep at a time. Usually, one shepherd led the way with a red flag on a long stick, as a warning to other road users, and sometimes there was also a sweeper with a similar flag. They reminded me of the little plastic flag I used to have on my bicycle as a kid. Involuntarily, I smiled.

The farther I rode into Kyrgyzstan, the warmer it got, and it was fantastic to have regained feeling in my fingers. In Osh, I even swapped my warm, black jacket for the light gray mesh jacket. It felt like I'd ridden from a chest freezer into a warm, tropical paradise in a matter of days. I reveled in the warmth and the sight of the beautiful mountains alongside rivers and lakes in the same shades of turquoise the river Panj had often had. Just like in Tajikistan, lunch along the way wasn't an easy task. I came across small shops at the side of the road, but they only sold soda and sweet candy. Once again, I was about to carry on without eating anything, but I decided to try one last shop.

"Hi," I said, addressing the guy behind the counter in English. "Do you have anything to eat?" Behind him stood tall shelves full of soft drinks, and I knew my prospects were bleak.

"Hi, welcome," he said, and then: "To eat?" He wore a black T-shirt and a red cap.

"A sandwich or..." I suggested. A young girl, probably his daughter, said something to him in Kyrgyz. "Sandwich?" he repeated, and then emerged from behind the counter. To my surprise, he produced a plate of pancakes. I couldn't believe my luck. Pancakes in Kyrgyzstan—I hadn't seen that coming. I sat down at a table in the store and dug in. I immediately stuffed such a big chunk into my mouth that it took me a moment to respond when he asked me where I was from.

With my mouth still full, I said: "From Holland."

"Amsterdam," he said. And then: "Robben."

As it turned out, Arjen Robben wasn't just beloved in Iran, but very much so in Kyrgyzstan too. We undoubtedly would have talked some more, had I not been so consumed by the pancakes that he just left me alone.

The warmth near Osh was short-lived, and on my way to Bishkek, the capital of Kyrgyzstan, I climbed to 9,840 feet in altitude, back into the freezer. A thick layer of snow covered the landscape like a smooth white blanket, but the road was thankfully dry and snow-free. It was a magical scene, and just like when I exited the Anzob Tunnel, I loved the sight of the snow. In Iran and Tajikistan, snow on the dirt roads had made me anxious, but now, riding on the spotless paved road, I felt enchanted by the winter scenery. As soon as I was over the mountain pass, the road began to descend and I left the snow behind once more. After a while, I started to notice some food stalls on the side of the road. Curious as to what they sold, I stopped by one of the stalls, parked Basanti and walked toward it. Two women stood within, both wearing long, warm tunics, with red scarves tied around their heads.

"What is this?" I said out loud, more to myself than to the women. I pointed at one of the plastic bags with big white balls in it.

"*Kurut,*" one of the women replied, but that didn't ring any bells.

"What is it," I asked again.

"Five, five," said the women, holding up five fingers.

Eventually I managed to convey the message that I only wanted to try one.

While they asked me where I was from, they handed me one of the white balls.

I tentatively took a small bite. Immediately, I realized this was a mistake. I wasn't quite sure what it was I had in my mouth, but it tasted like hardened milk that had passed its expiration date. Much later, I found out that this first impression had been pretty accurate. What had been melting on my tongue was made of fermented sheep's milk. The milk was salted and dried until it gained a hard, grainy texture, after which spices were added. *Kurut* was a popular snack in Kyrgyzstan because it had a long shelf life and didn't require refrigeration.

"I don't like it," I said, my lip curled in disgust.

I laughed awkwardly and then I did the unthinkable: I spit the gross, sour, dried-out milk onto the ground. There was no way I could hold it in. This was probably the biggest insult I had ever dished out in a foreign country.

Thankfully, the two women found this to be a rather hilarious scene, more amused than insulted. I chatted with them for a while longer and we introduced ourselves.

"Your name," asked one of the women, both of whom were called Aysan.

"Noraly," I said.

They echoed my name in surprise. "Noraly?"

I nodded. When I heard the names of the children who had started to emerge from behind the table, I understood why. One of the little boys turned out to be a Nurali, and I laughed and shook his little hand. Then I said goodbye to the women and their children and moved on.

That evening, as I was dragging my luggage from Basanti to my hotel room, I realized that I was in Kyrgyzstan, which meant I'd reached my goal once again, the one I'd set out in Malaysia months earlier. For the second time, I was facing the reality of having to turn around and ride back to India to return Basanti. But after all this time, I refused to entertain the thought of saying goodbye to my loyal friend for long. Frankly, there wasn't the tiniest part of me that even considered it. I would just have to lose the security deposit for the Carnet de Passage. I couldn't quite picture Mr. Dossa pushing the stacks of cash across the table toward me this time, anyway.

Alright, that settled it. I wouldn't be going back to India. All I needed was a new plan. I hunched over the map to study a new route, just as I'd done back in Kuala Lumpur, when my phone vibrated.

A message from my mum: "Hey sweet Noor! How are you? Riding still going okay?"

I reread the message a couple of times and glanced back at the map. Why couldn't I just ride all the way back to the Netherlands? I didn't see why not. In terms of picking a country, that seemed like a logical destination; my native country wasn't such a strange choice. I could import Basanti, and once she had Dutch plates, I'd be able to keep her. Then she would forever be mine. My eyes followed the line over the map I'd have to travel. First I'd have to cross Kazakhstan, then around the Caspian Sea through Russia and presto: I could ride straight into Europe via Turkey.

Chapter 12

Silent Loneliness

Miles: 13,420

From Bishkek, it was a short hop to the border with Kazakhstan. The shipment of motorcycle parts I'd ordered had arrived in Almaty in the meantime, and it was as though the new steering head bearings pulled me toward them like a magnet. The first few miles on Kazakh soil gave me a strange feeling of recognition. Even though I hadn't been in this exact place before, I knew Kazakhstan pretty well. I had worked on the Caspian Sea for a year, on Kazakh waters, and regularly spent time in Aktau—a city on mainland Kazakhstan.

I felt I'd been sent there more or less as punishment. The dredging company was large and employed nearly five thousand people, so there were always dozens of projects running at once, spread across almost the entire world. I had been working as a superintendent on a harbor project in Rio de Janeiro for nine months, staying in a gorgeous apartment a stone's throw from the famous Ipanema beach. When I asked for a transfer during the Zika virus outbreak in Brazil, I'd been sent elsewhere. It seemed my ungratefulness at being allowed to work somewhere as beautiful as Rio de Janeiro was rewarded with an assignment to the least desired project: Prorva, in Kazakhstan. The Prorva project meant dredging a forty-three-mile-long channel straight through the Caspian Sea. The dredged material was then used to build artificial islands on either side of the channel. They'd successfully done similar works in the Middle East, including off the coast of Dubai and in Saudi Arabia.

I wound up working on the islands of dredged sand and mud, which I had to make sure were built in the correct shape and dimensions, with the help of a small army of Kazakh employees. With large cranes and bulldozers, we worked day and night, twenty-four hours a day, seven days a week. For six consecutive weeks I worked fourteen hours a day, every day. We slept on board small, decades-old river cruise ships that now served as floating hotels. I had a tiny cabin on one of the ships, which I, thanks to the lack of women on the project, at least didn't have to share with anyone.

The summers were stinking hot and the winters horribly cold. There was no land to be seen except our homemade islands, drinking alcohol was prohibited, and there was nothing to do there but work. This had given the project a bad reputation, but against all odds, I loved it there. I could leave it to the Kazakhs to make sure no two days were the same, and that there was always some drama going on somewhere. A handful of them were genuinely great operators, but the majority of the men operating the bulldozers and excavators only had "tractor driver" listed as relevant experience on their resume. It was extremely dangerous and hilarious at the same time, the way they operated those huge machines. One moment they'd manage to bury their entire crane in quicksand, with only the top of the cabin still sticking out, and the next they'd accidentally run a bulldozer over the egg-filled nest of a protected seagull, getting us in trouble with environmentalists. They stole everything in sight, from cartons of cookies and tea to the first-aid kits on the excavators, sausages from the kitchen, and even entire barrels of oil from the mainland site in the village of Bautino. They made it a full-time job for me to constantly reorder everything that had been stolen, and I was perpetually at odds with health and safety officers over yet another missing first-aid kit on a machine. Once, a twelve-foot shipping container with safety gear was completely cleared out. The culprits were never found, but in the following weeks, half of Bautino strutted around in high-vis orange jackets and almost every man you saw wore a hard hat. I almost felt like I was at the Kazakhstan edition of Paris Fashion Week. Those men managed to keep me busy, drive project leaders to despair, and jeopardize the profitability of the project. It was chaos, but the time flew by.

I had a sneaking suspicion that my experience with the Kazakhs would be different this time, but in what way, I didn't yet know. I briefly swung by an exchange office in Almaty to exchange the one thousand Kyrgyz som I had left, and while I was there, I also exchanged fifty American dollars. Now I had a small stack of Kazakh tenge, and I could get gas. I thought about the service for Basanti I would have to arrange here, and the fact that the spare tires I'd been lugging around for almost 6,900 miles would soon be around her wheels instead of on top of my luggage. I felt pretty stupid, riding around with the two awkwardly tied-down spare tires that I'd brought all the way from Malaysia. It had been totally unnecessary and in most countries probably prohibited. Especially because I was going to change my tires in a city where I'd easily be able to find local ones. I had sort of expected them to be worn out somewhere halfway down the Pamir, where I wouldn't have been able to find new tires. I resolved not to tell the mechanics that would be working on Basanti that I had carried these tires in and out of seven countries and countless guesthouse rooms.

I checked in at a hostel in Almaty, where the accommodating guy who worked there shook up their entire planning to free up a bed for me. The hostel was completely booked, with a wide variety of travelers and backpackers, but nobody had come there on a motorcycle or by car. I had always felt at home amongst other travelers, but here I stuck out like a sore thumb. This crowd was dressed in trendy clothes, with funky hats and bright white sneakers, or accessorized with jewelry from exotic places. I was dirty and had, besides my muddy motorcycle gear, only one worn-out pair of jeans to wear. I hadn't ridden on an unpaved road since leaving Tajikistan, and yet everything was still dirty. No matter how hard I scrubbed and cleaned, the Pamir dirt didn't want to let go yet. It was as though I'd come riding out of an entirely different dimension from the people with whom I shared a room. It wasn't quite as if they were walking around me in a wide arc, but it felt like they were.

The next morning, I checked out and moved to a private room I rented from a young Kazakh. I preferred being alone over feeling like a misfit in a group. Once I'd hauled my things into the room, I got back onto Basanti and rode to the KTM dealership, because there was no Royal Enfield dealership in Almaty. But this place had the best reputation in town anyway.

It was only once I stepped foot inside the showroom that I noticed how big and fancy it was. The floor shone, as did the collection of motorcycles on display. It had slipped my mind how modern the big cities in Kazakhstan were. Sergey, one of the mechanics, was already waiting for me. I'd been in touch with him for a while about the parcel of motorcycle parts I'd had shipped, so he knew I was coming. We immediately got to work.

While his coworker started blasting the mud off Basanti outside with a pressure washer, I walked around the showroom. The gear on display looked so shiny and new that I wanted to buy it all. Everything I was wearing was either ripped or almost worn to threads, and though that hadn't really concerned me up to that point, seeing all those shiny new things suddenly made me realize how shabby I looked. When I inspected the racks more closely, I realized that, frustratingly, almost all of the clothing was only available in large men's sizes. There probably weren't a lot of women in Kazakhstan who rode motorcycles. None of it fit me. I eventually found a pair of leather motorcycle boots in a size 9.5 that had a snug fit, and I hugged the box tightly against me. These were coming with me.

My Ducati boots, which I'd first brought to India and which I'd climbed that mountain in Iran with, were now truly out of commission. The woodstove in the Tajik border office on the Kyzyl Art Pass had dealt them the final blow. In an attempt to dry and warm up my boots, the guard had placed them too close to the stove and unintentionally scorched them. These new leather boots, just like the Ducatis, were meant for wearing with street bikes: to ride around the city, commute, and other normal city behavior. They were absolutely not suited for what I was about to do in them. But I had plunged into the world of adventurous motorcycling completely blind, oblivious to what you were supposed to wear. I paid for the new boots, and the sales attendant asked me what I wanted to do with my old ones.

"Oh, just get rid of them," I said casually.

He nodded and disappeared into a dark room behind the counter.

I almost called after him, demanding to know what on earth he was doing with my boots. Suddenly, I regretted giving them away like that. Somehow, they had become symbolic of my lowest points. They had played crucial roles in the moments when things had been so incredibly difficult. Those were the moments that popped back in my mind when I looked at them. They didn't remind me of the thousands of miles that had gone off without any issues, but of the times when they'd tormented me. Part of me was afraid that throwing away those boots would also wipe away all those memories. I would be left with just the rosy memories of times when all went well and easy, and I didn't want that. It had been the hardships on the Pamir that had given me that "Pamir high." It had been the tears of relief at seeing the Iranian couple that had made the endless trek up the mountain worth it. It felt like my journey only had meaning because I'd had to go to so much trouble to complete it. And as if that meaning had somehow accumulated in a pair of worn-out motorcycle boots.

The mechanics worked all day long and replaced everything that needed replacing. I had skipped two services because I hadn't been able to find a mechanic or because the spare parts weren't available, so this one was long overdue.

When I rolled out of the dealership with a fixed-up Basanti at the end of the afternoon, Sergey closed the doors behind me. They had managed to finish just before closing time, and I rode into the falling dusk with a sense of relief. I was ready for the next few thousand miles: all the way across the Kazakh steppes.

But I hadn't even gone 2 miles toward my room when all the lights suddenly started blinking. Not just on the dashboard—my headlights joined in too. My bike had turned into a Christmas tree on wheels and I stopped, startled.

I turned the key in the ignition and stared perplexedly at the dashboard. I had no clue what was going on. Hadn't I just had her fully serviced? I turned the key back and hoped for a miracle. This strategy had sometimes worked for me in the past when dealing with computer problems. I would turn them off, turn them back on, and then everything would work again. My lack of motorcycle knowledge became painfully clear to me once again when I pressed the start button and nothing happened.

It was as if Basanti looked at me and said: "You have no idea what you're doing, do you?"

I sighed. A man who had been watching me from a distance came walking toward me.

"Not working?" he asked in English. I shook my head. "Probably the battery," he said.

"But I just came from a dealership, surely that can't be it?" As it turns out, I have issues trusting other people's diagnoses when it came to my motorcycle. But he insisted and explained what I had to do. "Second gear, stand on the pegs, and when you start the engine, quickly sit down so there's pressure on the rear wheel. I'll push."

Although his English was excellent, he might as well have been speaking Kazakh, that's how little I understood how this was supposed to work. I tried to follow his instructions as well as I could, and lo and behold, she started on the third try. I whooped and gave him a thumbs-up as I kept riding, worried the engine would stall again. While I was still internally debating if I was better off riding back to my room or back to the closed motorcycle dealership, all the lights began flickering again and the engine cut out once more. Luckily I knew what to do now, and I waved at the nearest man on the sidewalk.

"Would you mind pushing me?" I asked.

Just like the previous passerby, he was more than happy to give me a little push, and within a minute I was back on my way. My happiness was short-lived this time as well. And when I had found my third victim to push me, the trick had stopped working. I couldn't get Basanti back to life anymore, and I dismounted, feeling disillusioned. It had gotten dark by now, with the streetlights casting a weak glow onto the road. The only thing I could think to do was to push her back to the dealership. It was closer than my hotel and if I didn't go now, I would still have to do it tomorrow morning from even farther away. I glanced down at my brand-new motorcycle boots. For a moment, I felt like an idiot for struggling to say goodbye to my old boots just a few hours earlier. Apparently I didn't need them to get myself into trouble after all. I tapped Basanti into neutral with my foot and started pushing.

Beads of sweat began to form on my back and then trickle in a single stream directly down my spine and into my pants. For the umpteenth time on this journey, I cursed Royal Enfield for making such a ridiculously heavy motorcycle. How did they manage to make a single-cylinder, 411 cc motorcycle weigh more than 440 pounds? She may have been built like an indestructible tank, but as far as I was concerned, she could have stood to lose a few pounds.

Even in neutral gear, it took me an incredible amount of force to push the behemoth along. When I had left the dealership I hadn't noticed the road gradually descending, but now that I had to push everything back up a couple of miles, it felt like I was climbing a mountain. I stopped for a moment and kicked out the side stand. I took my phone out of my pocket to see where I was. I could go straight ahead from here, or I could take a shortcut through a side street. Then I'd only have to push another half mile to the KTM dealership. I decided to take the shortcut and pushed Basanti in the direction of a small alleyway. It was even darker there than on the street, and I suddenly felt vulnerable. The smell of danger filled my nostrils. Just like that day in the mountains of Tajikistan, I felt like I was being watched. With feigned nonchalance, I slowly turned my head and peered into the dark. I saw nobody and heard nothing over my own noisy breathing. I didn't like the dark. I was partially night-blind, and even though I'd never had an official diagnosis, I was aware of my struggle to see clearly after sundown. It was the main reason why I often rushed to my destination like a madwoman, to arrive in the afternoon; I absolutely did not want to ride in the dark.

I got my first pair of glasses when I was just seven years old, and in the years that followed my eyesight quickly further deteriorated. It went so fast that I needed stronger lenses every few months. My parents had to work like crazy to afford new sets of expensive lenses, which would disappear into the trash just three months later. I hated those glasses with a passion. When I was fifteen, I was finally old enough for contact lenses, but my eyesight was so bad that I still needed glasses to find my bed after taking out my contacts in the bathroom.

Although I knew the dealership had already closed by now, the pace I pushed on was as if I could still make it just before they cleared out. To distract myself from the fact that I was on my own pushing my motorcycle through a dark alley in the capital of Kazakhstan, I focused only on the thought of getting there. What I'd do with Basanti once I got there was another matter.

From the day I'd left Delhi I'd had to learn, more than ever before, to rely on myself. There was no other option. Without anyone by my side to give me a pep talk if I threw in the towel, I was the one who had to solve the day-to-day issues, put together the logistical jigsaw puzzle, keep my spirits up, and maintain order over the whole shebang while on the road. When I was sick, nobody would come to my rescue and put a damp cloth on my forehead or make me a cup of soup. It had been like this for months, but on that day in Kazakhstan, the realization of it hit me in a new way, and one that I would rather not have experienced.

I panted and wheezed and wanted nothing more than to take off my helmet. But I needed both hands to push the bike and didn't dare dangle the helmet on one of the mirrors. If it fell on the ground, an inner shell could break and the helmet would, officially speaking, no longer be safe. I conveniently forgot that it had come bouncing out of my hands twice already in the past few months, and that there probably wasn't much left of the inner shell anyway.

Although the alley looked ominous in the dark, thankfully nobody else had felt the need to be there at the same time as me. I rolled out onto the other side and saw the orange lamps of the KTM dealership light up in the distance. Seeing those lights gave me renewed energy and I quickened my step until Basanti started to roll so fast that I had to trot beside her to keep up. We both came to a stop in front of the tall, pointy fence and I blankly looked at it for a moment. I hadn't considered the possibility of there being a fence, and one at quite a large distance from the dealership. I looked around but didn't see anywhere else to safely park Basanti. I had no choice but to park her here, outside of the fence. I took the motorcycle cover out of the pannier and pulled it over the bike, hoping she wouldn't draw any unwanted attention from under the cover, and that she'd still be here in the morning.

I looked at my phone, and by some miracle I still had the taxi app downloaded from when I'd worked in Kazakhstan years earlier. Within five minutes, an old Lada (*What else*, I thought) rolled past the fence and I got in. The driver said nothing and we sat in the car in silence until he dropped me off at my room. That night, I lay in bed with my stomach in knots and a head full of worries. I thought about Basanti, parked all alone in the dark by that abandoned road in Almaty. Apart from the flight between Kuala Lumpur and Oman, we had never been so far apart.

"Don't be silly," I said out loud. I behaved as if my motorcycle was an extension of myself, like I was supposed to have her by my side at all times. Maybe I never should have named her, I thought. I'd probably be sleeping better if I hadn't.

After a restless night, I took a taxi back to the motorcycle dealership first thing in the morning. As we neared the fence, my nose was glued to the car window to try to see if she was still there. I breathed a sigh of relief when I saw the motorcycle cover with the silhouette of an Enfield underneath. She was still there. I waited outside for a while until Sergey arrived, and he raised both eyebrows in surprise when he saw me.

"Not good?"

"Not good," I said.

He opened the padlock that hung around the fence and swung it open.

"Come, come," he said, beckoning me onto the lot.

I pushed Basanti inside, right up to the gate of the workshop.

"What's the problem?" asked Sergey. I started rambling incoherently about Christmas trees and dark alleyways in Almaty. He nodded and left me in the store with a cup of coffee while he disappeared into the workshop. I took small sips of the coffee until he reappeared not much later and casually said: "All sorted. It was just a broken fuse."

The next day, I left Almaty with mixed feelings. I wanted to leave the city as quickly as possible, back into vast nature, but the thought of what lay ahead filled me with dread. Before I'd arrive at the Russian border, there would be 2,175 miles of Kazakh steppe ahead of me. This would be the most mind-numbing, least stimulating part of my journey, and I wasn't exactly looking forward to it. I had decided to apply for a transit visa for Russia, the only Russian visa I could organize in Kazakhstan. I couldn't get a tourist visa in Almaty. That meant I'd have to get a move on to make it to the Russian border in time, and then ride through Russia to Georgia within the length of the transit visa. This route allowed me to go around the Caspian Sea, so at least I wouldn't have to cross it on an unreliable ferry.

The first few hundred miles after leaving Almaty, I was relishing riding my motorcycle on quiet roads without traffic lights, set against sprawling fields full of wildflowers. This area was flat, and I felt like I could see dozens of miles ahead before the road finally disappeared behind the horizon. After a few days of keeping up the pace, I noticed that the terrain was getting more and more arid. The temperature rose a degree or so every fifty miles. Instead of cars, I only saw camels on the road.

I stopped at a small store on the side of the road. I bought a bar of chocolate, which on further inspection turned out to be six months past its expiration date, and a can of Coke. I usually wasn't a fan of soda, but the emptiness of the steppe had awakened all kinds of food fantasies in me. I thought about peanut butter with chocolate sprinkles, lasagna made from a Jamie Oliver recipe, fat slices of Dutch cheese. I yearned for Greek yogurt with muesli and a baguette with tomato soup. If I concentrated hard enough, I could almost taste the flavor of a fresh stroopwafel on my tongue. And I'd have a strong cup of coffee to go with it. Coffee like a good barista prepares it. All they drank in

Kazakhstan was tea. The Kazakhs drank so much tea that I sometimes wondered how they had time left to do anything else.

As I crossed the steppe, I rode so many consecutive hours in a day that at night I dreamt I was still on my motorcycle. No matter how tightly my eyes were squeezed shut, I still saw the endless plains pass me by. The steppe, my motorcycle, and I were so intertwined that it was all I saw and did. A feeling of loneliness had been slumbering in the background for a while by this point, but it grew stronger with every mile I traveled through Kazakhstan. This loneliness reminded me of being in that dark tunnel in Tajikistan, where the end simply refused to come into sight. The monotony of the scenery was a vivid reflection of my own loneliness. The landscape was empty, barren, and dry, and so was I on the inside.

I would meet a handful of people every day, at the gas stations or hotels, but the language barrier stood in the way of any real connection. We didn't get much further than "hello," "how are you," and "good." Sometimes I thought I could read more in the eyes of the Kazakhs, but maybe that was just my imagination. I longed so intensely for a real conversation that I started talking out loud to Basanti, and to myself, too. Without people around me to talk to, loneliness was always ready to strike, and it was driving me mad. Was this the price I paid for freedom?

Just like when my journey began, months earlier, I was plagued by intruding thoughts. I would often start the day by thinking about where I would go that day and pondering all the countries I wanted to visit next. But as the day went by, and the landscape remained flat, barren and empty, I would no longer think ahead but to the past. Back to my broken relationship, the betrayal, and everything I'd lost. Like stubborn heartburn, it all came back up.

Although I tried to look at the vast landscape around me, the image of a single photograph kept appearing before my eyes instead. The framed photograph of him and her together at work, which he had placed smack-dab in the middle of our living room. They stood close together, laughing as they leaned against a company car. At the time, he told me she'd given him the photograph as a gift, but I later found out that he'd printed it himself, framed it, and placed it in our living room. Every time I walked into our house, that photo was the first thing I saw. He was cheating on me with his coworker and went ahead and put a picture of them two in the house we'd built together. Who does that? Was this some kind of sick psychological game, or was he subconsciously trying to tell me his big secret?

It was the most painful thing anyone had ever done to me, and I wondered if that said more about him or about how pain-free my life had been up to that point. I wondered, but some part of me already knew the answer. I had been born into a loving family, in a peaceful and wealthy country. There are people who have to risk their lives in ramshackle boats because in their own country bombs are quite literally flying over their heads. My emotional pain was nothing compared to the suffering of these people. And yet I kept thinking about that picture, until I felt like a complete moron for the way I was torturing myself with it. I tried to force myself to think about something else. Sometimes, a song would spontaneously get stuck in my head. Usually not a full song—only fragments of one. It would play over and over again in a relentless loop, without ever switching to another song. I would try to think of another song and tempt it to stick around in my head for a bit, but it never worked.

I stopped at a restaurant by the side of the deserted road to buy water. I pushed aside the two plastic flaps that hung in the doorway and stepped inside. I spotted a small shop in the corner of the restaurant.

"Hello," I greeted the older woman behind the counter. I smiled at her. She wore a light purple headscarf and a dark purple tunic. "Water?" I asked in Russian, pointing behind her. In front of the wall with hideous flowered wallpaper stood a row of fridges with a variety of drinks.

"Gas, no gas?"

"No gas," I said, shaking my head.

The woman said something and gestured at a low fridge on my side of the counter.

I took out a large bottle of water and she said: "Two hundred tenge." I gave her a one thousand tenge bill.

"Do you have anything smaller? Don't you have two hundred tenge?"

"Maybe," I muttered, sticking my hand deep into my pants pocket.

A handful of change popped out, and the woman nodded approvingly. "You have it, you have it." I placed two coins on the counter and she gave me my one thousand tenge bill back. She opened a drawer and slid the two coins inside.

"Where are you going? That way, or that way?" I pointed in the right direction. "You alone?" she asked then.

"Alone," I confirmed for the thousandth time. I usually didn't mind telling people that I was traveling by myself. But lately, it felt as though everyone took every opportunity to grab me by the head and harshly rub my nose into the fact that I was indeed all alone. I didn't feel like elaborating any further on the matter, so I grabbed the bottle of water and strolled outside.

"Goodbye," I said.

I put the change back into my pocket and unscrewed the cap of the water bottle. While I drank and stared at Basanti, an uncomfortable feeling settled on me. I couldn't quite put my finger on what it was. It felt like homesickness, but I didn't know if I was homesick for what lay behind me, the dramatic scenery of Tajikistan and the real adventure, or homesick for something familiar. Something that lay ahead and almost felt within reach: Europe. It felt like I was stuck in a vacuum, trapped between the spectacular, dangerous mountains of Central Asia and my boring but safe home continent.

I emptied the water I couldn't drink right away into my backpack reservoir so I could keep drinking as I rode. I grabbed my helmet, put it on, and climbed back onto the seat. In Iran, I had been convinced that my body had adapted to the long hours on the motorcycle. I thought my butt and back were so strong and muscular by now that nothing could harm them anymore. But no matter how strong I thought I was, I was taken down by the endless plains of Kazakhstan. The aches I'd had in India and well into Thailand had returned with a vengeance. My left shoulder was so sore that most of the time I held it slack against my body. My neck was so stiff that my traps had swelled and I was starting to look like a bodybuilder. My butt may have been muscular, but my muscles were as bruised as a ripe banana.

When I approached the halfway point of my ride through Kazakhstan, I rode past Baikonur. It was the most exciting place for miles and the closer I got, the more attention I paid to the sky. I rode past the space center where they launched manned and unmanned rockets. With a bit of luck, I might be able to see one blast off. I couldn't enter Baikonur because it wasn't Kazakh territory but, in fact, a Russian enclave, and my Russian transit visa wasn't valid there. But even from a distance I found it fascinating to be so close to this site, which had been kept a secret for so long.

Baikonur was built in the fifties during the height of the Cold War. The Soviets built the secret space center and called it Baikonur to throw off the West and make them think the location was near the mining town of Baikonur. After the Soviet Union collapsed and Kazakhstan gained independence, it took some time before they figured out what to do with the facility. This left the unfortunate Russian cosmonaut Sergei Krikalev stuck in space for an extra couple of months, while Russia and Kazakhstan negotiated over the future of Baikonur. A solution was reached with a lease agreement that allowed the Russians to lease the Baikonur Cosmic Dream for more than one hundred million dollars a year. And thus, it became a special Russian enclave within Kazakhstan from which satellites, scientific missions, and interplanetary probes were launched.

–

I suddenly realized that I hadn't eaten anything for hours and was starving. I stopped at a roadside restaurant not far outside Baikonur, looking for food. While I waited for my order, I tried to pry some more information about the rockets out of the restaurant staff. The two women who worked there didn't say much, and instead gestured for me to go outside and have a look for myself. My interest sparked, I went back out, and as I walked around the building, I saw the skeletons of rockets in the desert behind the restaurant. Their insides were completely scorched and the material that had once covered them hung down in loose strips. I didn't have the slightest clue what the debris once belonged to, but it felt surreal to be walking right through a rocket part in the desert of Kazakhstan. I chuckled. A year ago I could never have imagined I would be standing here right now. Never. I wandered around for a while, wondering where the rocket these parts came from had gone to. Then I went back inside and tucked into a plate of warm dumplings.

I had 137 miles to go to Aralsk, where I wanted to spend the night. To kill time, I played a game in my head that my family used to play in the car. I thought of the name of an animal, and the last letter of that word had to be the first letter of the next animal. Donkey, yak, kangaroo, otter, raccoon. When I couldn't think of any more animals in Dutch, I decided to add a new rule and allowed myself to use English names as well. Only the game was not nearly as fun on my own, and I stopped when I couldn't come up with anything else after rhinoceros.

I was glad when I saw the town of Aralsk emerge in the distance. Aralsk was originally located right on the shores of the Aral Sea, but nowadays the fishing boats were found on the bottom of the seafloor. There was almost nothing left of the Aral Sea. During Soviet times, the two rivers that fed into it—the Amu Darya and the Syr Darya—had been diverted. The water was used to irrigate large-scale cotton plantations, causing the lake to dry up almost entirely, leaving behind a vast area of salt flats and salt deposits. When Kazakhstan gained independence, dams were built to lead the water from the two rivers back to the lake. The water level had risen a little since then, but when I rode into Aralsk harbor, I saw the boats still lying abandoned in a dry Aral Sea. It was a somber sight, and the excitement I had felt earlier that day while walking between the rocket debris faded into the background. I was more than ready to leave Kazakhstan, but I was more than 1,000 miles away from reaching the Russian border.

So I pushed on to Aktobe, traveling 383 miles in a single day: a new record. All day long, I entertained myself with fantasies about a faster, more powerful, more comfortable, completely protected-from-the-wind superbike. One of those motorcycles with 120 horsepower, four cylinders, and cruise control. And then: mind in neutral, speedometer at 150. In real life, I wasn't riding one of those at all. Instead, I plodded along on my single-cylinder with less than 25 horsepower, over a smooth asphalt road that just begged to be torn up. Basanti had successfully carried me over all the narrow mountain paths and bumpy roads in Asia and the Middle East, but now I desperately wished I was riding a motorcycle that could go just a little faster.

PART 3

Nobody would have thought we'd come this far, including me.

Chapter 13

Three Loop-de-Loops

Miles: 15,845

All this time, it seemed the Kazakh steppe would just never end, but once I'd passed Atyrau and arrived at the Russian border, I found myself out of Kazakhstan in the blink of an eye. In just over an hour, I had wrapped up Kazakhstan's immigration and customs and been stamped into Russia. I couldn't believe it! Although the scenery was the same on the Russian side, I was excited, the way I always was whenever I rode into a different country. I immediately set course for the city of Astrakhan and everything went smoothly, until I reached the river Buzan at the village of Krasnyi Yar. I saw some kind of toll booth and realized I had to pay to cross here. Except that I didn't have any Russian rubles yet. There hadn't been any money changers at the border willing to trade with me in a sketchy corner somewhere. All I had on me in cash were Kazakh tenge and American dollars. I parked Basanti next to a moped and walked into a small restaurant, hoping they'd be willing to exchange some cash.

"Ruble? Tenge?" I asked the woman behind the counter of the restaurant. With my hands I mimed an exchange of some sort. She looked at me and said nothing. A younger man sitting at a table with a cup of tea called out: "Bank, bank."

"Sure, bank, that works," I said. "Where can I find a bank?"

He proceeded to give me directions in rapid Russian, pointing left and right in the air a few times. My facial expression most likely spoke for itself, and he knocked back his last mouthful of tea and tapped me on the shoulder. I followed him outside and he walked up to the blue moped beside which I'd parked Basanti. I quickly put on my helmet, pulled my gloves back on, and started the engine. I followed him for a while, and we zigzagged through the village until he slowed down at a tall, stately building: the bank.

"Thanks," I shouted, and the young man on the moped took off.

Right when I was about to walk up the steps that led to the bank's entrance, an older woman, who had some trouble walking, came down. She was holding a cane to assist her. She stopped when she saw me.

"Hello," she called out.

"Hello," I said, and smiled at her. I loved it when strangers on the streets greeted me out of nowhere.

"How are you?" she asked.

"Good, and you?" She nodded and continued down the steps.

I entered the bank, exchanged my last tenge for rubles, and came back outside. While I walked back to Basanti, I thought about the guy on the moped and the woman with the cane. I had been in Russia for less than a day, and already I was being greeted and helped by complete strangers. In that sense, the people here hadn't changed a bit in recent years.

I thought back to my first visit to Russia five years earlier. I had just finished a project in the harbor of Tangier, Morocco, and had negotiated six weeks of leave. I needed those six weeks, because I wanted to take the Trans-Siberian Express. From Saint Petersburg, I hoped to travel by train via Moscow and then ever eastward to Siberia. There, I planned to transfer to the Trans-Mongolian Express and follow that all the way to Beijing in China.

The idea of traveling through all of Russia by train and ending up in China had been in my head for years. I'd first heard about it from my cousin Jeroen. He did it with a friend of his, and it was the most adventurous thing anyone from our family had done up to that point. He had boarded the train in Moscow and not gotten off until two weeks later in Beijing. He had regaled the entire family with what it was like on board the train, how there were all kinds of merchants at the stations trying to sell food through the windows and how he'd watched the trees pass by. I found his story fascinating and listened to it with rapt attention. The only thing I hadn't understood was why someone would want to spend two full weeks aboard a train. So from that moment on I had toyed with the idea of doing the same trip, only spreading it across six weeks so I could hop off the train at various places and have time to explore them before catching the next train.

I'd flown to Saint Petersburg and wandered the city for a few days. I visited the Church of the Savior on Spilled Blood, which had been built in commemoration of the murder of Emperor Alexander II. It was the most impressive building I had ever seen. I stared open-mouthed at the Russian-orthodox architecture on the outside, with its colorful domes and gold crosses. The interior consisted of eighty thousand square feet of unbelievably beautiful mosaics that depicted various stories from the Bible. It had taken twenty-four years to build, but that still seemed like a rush job to me considering the amount of work it must have been. I visited the Zoological Museum, which even had a mammoth on display. A real mammoth! Then I wandered over to the museum next door, the Kunstkamera, founded by Peter the Great in 1704. He was an emperor of Russia who took an interest in scientific research and collected anthropological artifacts. I'd stared in horror at rows of jars containing fetuses and babies in formaldehyde with the most gruesome deformities and birth defects. Feeling sick, I made my way outside, having lost the urge to visit museums. I took the night train to Moscow the next day.

There, I had strolled across Red Square, gazed at the Kremlin, and looked at Lenin's embalmed body in the mausoleum where he'd been lying in state for a full century. That was simply what you were supposed to do as a tourist in Moscow. I decided then that it was time to leave for Siberia. I boarded the train to Kungur, which would be my first properly long train journey through Russia: it would take eighteen hours. Russian passengers in my car tried to start conversation, and armed with a pocket dictionary we got along just fine. I feel like this train journey was the first time I truly learned to connect with strangers, language barrier or not. Another passenger had, when it was his stop to get out, quickly pressed two coins into my hands. Surprised, I'd stammered: *"Spassiba."* Thank you. When the doors closed again and the train slowly started to move, I opened my fist and looked at them. One coin was a modern ruble, but the other one was much older. I carefully examined it and after showing it to the Russian woman next to me, it turned out that he'd given me, to my astonishment, an imperial copper coin from 1738. He couldn't have known that I had collected coins from all over the world in neatly organized plastic binders since I was a kid. This complete stranger couldn't have given me a better goodbye present. Over the moon, I had wrapped my hand tightly around the small coin and had looked out of the window until the platform disappeared from sight.

A few days later, on the train somewhere halfway through Russia, things suddenly went south. I started to feel a little sick, and a strange rash appeared on my stomach, which itched terribly. I gently rubbed my finger over the bumps that appeared and tried to convince myself that it wasn't bedbugs. I was now practically living on different bunk beds on the trains and I didn't know how often the cabins were cleaned between occupants. I tried to make myself as comfortable as I could and get some sleep, but a few hours later I woke up with a horrible, explosive rash. My legs, arms, stomach, back, and bum felt like they were on fire and my skin was red-hot and swollen. Panicking, I clambered out of the sleeping compartment and barreled through the train. I found a train conductor and without saying a word, I rolled up my T-shirt and showed my burning hot stomach. She made no effort to hide her disgust, wrinkling her nose while she examined it for a moment. She said something, turned around, and dashed into the opposite direction, through the aisle. I was left alone, unsure what to do. I noticed people were staring at me and quickly pulled my T-shirt back down. With my head lowered and my gaze fixed on the floor, I rushed back to my bunk. To my relief, the conductor reappeared a few minutes later with two perfectly round pills in her hand. What a legend. As she pressed them into my hand, she briefly looked at me and nodded. I knocked back the pills with a mouthful of water, laid down, and tried not to think about the itching. Less than an hour later, the rash was completely gone. It turned out I was allergic to Russian trains.

When the train finally crossed the border into Mongolia, I left Russia with a different view of the people than I'd had before. Despite an arduous language barrier, the Russians I'd met had shown an interest in me, shared their food and drinks with me, and helped me when I'd needed them. And they had done it all nearly with indifference, as though it was nothing. The young man who had just escorted me to the bank was exactly the same. When I thanked him, he had just shrugged his shoulders, turned around, and carried on doing what he'd been doing.

In possession of Russian rubles, I rode toward the river in Kasnyi Yar. To my surprise there was no ferry or toll bridge, but instead a pontoon bridge that I needed to cross. With slight hesitation I carefully rode

Basanti onto the first pontoon. The Buzan was wide, and from what I could tell this floating bridge had to be at least a third of a mile long. So many parts had been attached to each other that the whole thing ominously bobbed up and down when I rode across it. I started to feel sick. At the time, I didn't realize that pontoon bridges were mostly used in wartime, so an army could quickly cross rivers. I also didn't know that Russia would use pontoon bridges like the one I was riding across in the invasion of Ukraine only three years later. All I was worrying about was the possibility of throwing up in my helmet, and the route I'd have to follow through Russia.

My Russian transit visa was valid for a week, which meant I didn't have much time to waste. Especially because I also wanted to maintain a margin of at least two days in case I unexpectedly found myself with engine trouble or other delays. That's why I preferred to take the shortest route toward Russia's border with Georgia. I'd studied the map for a while and considered various options. I saw that the shortest one ran closely along the coast of the Caspian Sea, through the Russian republic of Dagestan. Afterward, I'd have to turn toward the west and cross through the entirety of the republic of Chechnya to reach the Georgian border.

The Greater Caucasus mountain range began in southern Dagestan, and that was an area I was dying to see. I wanted to meet the Avars there, one of the largest ethnic groups in Dagestan. The language they spoke didn't resemble Russian at all, and contrary to the predominant Orthodox Christians in Russia, they were mostly Muslim. The problem with this route wasn't even about having to traverse Dagestan, although there were warnings of civil unrest, terrorism, and kidnappings there. The problem was mostly that after Dagestan, I'd have to go into Chechnya. This tiny republic was dwarfed by the massive size of Russia, but the Chechens had nonetheless made things difficult for the Russians for a long time, and at a high cost. When the Soviet Union collapsed, Chechnya immediately declared its independence, and both the president of Russia at the time, Boris Yeltsin, and its current president, Vladimir Putin, waged wars to annex Chechnya. Eventually Putin managed to put his confidant, Ramzan Kadyrov, at the head of Chechnya. I had understood that this Kadyrov had brought stability to the republic but ruled it like a cruel dictator. I decided in the end to completely stay away from both Dagestan and Chechnya.

Even if things were relatively stable there, the name Chechnya brought enough chilling war images to mind to urge me away.

So instead I rode west for a long time, through the republic Kalmykia, though I might as well have been still riding across the immeasurable steppes of Kazakhstan. This was no different: The boundless grasslands were occasionally interrupted by dried-up salt lakes, but other than that I saw nothing but emptiness. I had even less human interaction here than in Kazakhstan. The police checks weren't even manned by real people any longer, but now only consisted of flat cardboard signs with an image of a police car and an officer. At a gas station where I stopped, the attendant sat behind a closed door, and only after ringing twice did a small hatch open through which I could hand him the rubles for gas. I was preemptively beginning to pity the first poor soul who spoke good English who'd run into me. I felt an incessant stream of words bubbling up, about everything that had happened over the past few weeks that I hadn't been able to tell anyone about yet. I didn't know then that I'd meet a group of English-speaking travelers in Tbilisi, the capital of Georgia, who would all meet this fate. They didn't know that either—and perhaps that was for the best.

The next morning, I had a large breakfast of omelet with toast, cookies, and a small bowl of *kasha*, porridge made from boiled millet. From Elista, the capital of the autonomous Republic of Kalmykia where I'd spent the night, I wanted to ride to Stavropol. With fresh reluctance, I mounted Basanti and prepared myself for yet another day of mind-numbing, endless, flat steppe.

I had only just left when I came across not a fake, flat cardboard sign, but a real police checkpoint. With a black-and-white checked baton, a police officer gestured for me to stop. He wore an impressive, tall black police cap with a broad gold-colored brim, a white shirt, and navy pants.

"*Dobre den*," he greeted me. Good afternoon.

"*Dobre den*," I replied. He walked to the back of my motorcycle to inspect my license plate. I could tell by his face that my license plate didn't help him figure out what country the bike came from.

"India," I helped him.

"India?"

"Motorcycle from India, me from Holland," I tried to explain. He looked at me, amused.

"Document?" I handed him my passport. "Noraly?" He studied my passport.

"Yes," I said, nodding. I gave him the motorcycle registration papers.

"Is this a driver's license, or what?" he said in Russian. "Or is this a motorcycle document. And where is your driver's license?"

I didn't understand what he was saying and didn't respond. He switched to English. "Driver's license." All my documents were in order, and he gave me the signal that I was free to go. *Where are you going?* he wanted to know before I left.

"Georgia," I replied.

"Gruziya," he confirmed, using the Russian word for Georgia. "Safe travels."

I didn't meet or speak to anyone else until Stavropol. The last part of my ride through Russia brought me to the republics of Kabardino-Balkaria and North Ossetia-Alania. Until I'd studied the map to figure out my route, I'd had no idea that there were so many autonomous republics within Russia. I also didn't know that everything would get better once I reached Kabardino-Balkaria. Finally—*finally*—the flat-as-a-pancake terrain turned first into hills and then mountains. I was meeting more people—okay, I still wasn't having deep conversations, but I was easy to please at this point.

I passed through cute historic towns, came across excellent coffee and fresh salads and rode through woods for the first time in ages, where I inhaled the delicious smell of the trees as if my nose was a forest sommelier. "Ah, a sublime vintage of beech with just a hint of pine." Change was in the air.

The Greater Caucasus was an impressive mountain range that extended from the Caspian Sea to the Black Sea like a natural wall. The tallest mountain in Europe, the dormant volcano Mount Elbrus, was here. This mountain was even 2,744 feet taller than Mont Blanc, which was usually called the tallest mountain in Europe. The land border I crossed between Russia and Georgia was the only open land border between both countries, nestled within a narrow valley surrounded by towering mountains. As the only border crossing, it wasn't surprising that traffic was five lanes deep to exit Russia and five lanes deep to enter. While I waited in line for my turn, a man who had been watching me for a while approached.

"Georgia," he began in Russian, pointing at the jerrycan of fuel I'd screwed onto my bike. "No, no, fine. You have to fill your tank," he said, and pointed at the main tank of my motorcycle.

"Ah, okay," I said.

"Fine," he repeated. "You're not allowed to have jerrycans with you."

"That's not allowed?"

"Fine, Georgia will give you a fine. The jerrycan must be empty."

"We'll see," I said in English and laughed.

"I forgot English a long time ago," he replied in Russian.

I was grateful for his warning about a fine, but there wasn't much I could do about it. I wasn't going to get rid of my jerrycans because I might still need them, and I also didn't have a place to hide them on the motorcycle. I decided to just keep them where they were and see how far I got. As it turned out, nobody said anything about my jerrycans and I never got fined. Sometimes, all you need is just a healthy dose of luck.

After two hours of the usual border-crossing formalities, I found myself in Georgia. Meadows spread across the mountains like an immaculate stretch of pool felt, and I followed the winding road through the valleys toward Tbilisi.

I'd left my loneliness behind when I rode out of Russia. As soon as I entered the lot of the hostel in Tbilisi, I spotted two parked motorcycles and a car with a Dutch license plate. Travelers! I had found my victims. For days, a group of us exchanged stories and I behaved the most sociable since Dushanbe. And then something remarkable happened. I didn't need a visa for Georgia, so it wasn't a rush job to ride through the country like I'd had to in Russia. I had all the time in the world. But after I'd put my affairs in order in Tbilisi—Basanti needed another oil change after 3,100 miles—I rode straight out of Georgia and into Armenia.

At the time, I wasn't sure why I did so. All I knew then, was that I wanted to move forward and not draw a meandering line with three loop-de-loops across the map of Georgia. My first two days in Armenia, I rode together with a Swiss motorcyclist I'd met in Tbilisi, Toni, because he'd been turned away at the border of Azerbaijan and had decided to tag along to Armenia. I quickly realized that, despite all the loneliness I'd felt in Kazakhstan and Russia, I was still a solo traveler at heart and soul. Toni couldn't let me forget how wonderful it was to travel alone, and to be honest, I wasn't looking for someone who could. I had clearly fully recharged my social battery in Tbilisi, and now I was itching to continue my solo ride. But even once I was back to riding on my own, I still didn't take my time and thoroughly explore the country, even though my visa allowed for it. It took me a while to fully grasp why.

In India, I had realized the existence of turning points. Real turning points, that sprung from one single decision and completely changed the further course of one's life. There was that one day in 2010, when I sent an email from the town of Rishikesh in India to my professor at the university with the message that I wouldn't be returning to the Netherlands to finish my PhD research on isorenieratene, thereby abandoning a career in academics. That one email eventually led me, completely broke, to look for gold in Australia, and then my many subsequent wild adventures all over the world as a dredging superintendent. But I realized that perhaps the most important turning point of my life had now arrived. It had been a convergence of fate, the deliberate input of others, and my own free will, that I was standing here now. I knew that the betrayal, my boss trying to force me to work in the Netherlands, meeting Pankaj, and the invitation for the wedding in Kashmir had all been part of a new life as the filmmaker and motorcycle adventurer. It took me a long time—a really long time—to finally see that this was how it was meant to be: Basanti and me. The spark for adventure had always been there in my heart, but that little motorcycle had fed its flame and turned it into an inferno that wouldn't be going out anytime soon.

I finally understood what it was, that feeling I'd had back in Kazakhstan that I'd labeled homesickness. I couldn't be homesick for home, because I didn't have a house anymore. I wasn't homesick for my country, except maybe for a nice cheese sandwich. No, that wasn't it. So, what was it then?

From the moment I had changed my final destination for the third time—to the Netherlands—I was no longer going toward something, but now, I was going back. Instead of having a new goal on the horizon, riding toward some new place, filled with anticipation, I was returning. I was riding back to the continent I already knew, where I had visited almost every country once, or multiple times. Back to the familiar, back to what I had already been. I loved to reach my destination, but it was that feeling of going back instead of forward that was bothering me immensely.

At first, I still forced myself to keep exploring. To visit the tourist attractions and not neglect the back roads either. I had loved the mountains of Georgia and the hospitality of the Armenians, which strongly reminded me of that of the Iranians. But once I rode into Türkiye, I caught myself taking increasingly direct routes and sticking to the main roads more often and for longer. From time to time, I still had the occasional tense moment, even though I imagined myself safely back in Europe. At a gas station in Türkiye, I narrowly escaped the heavy thunderstorm that had been chasing me for a while, like some jet-black monster, and that eventually caught up to me with all its mighty force. In Montenegro, I misjudged what should have been a fun unpaved track and ended up on a path that was way too technical for my skill set. In Bosnia, I realized far too late that I'd turned onto a trail that was so overgrown that the risk of riding onto a land mine, a sad result of the war in the mid-nineties, was way too great to simply ignore. The highlights were the stunning rock formations of Meteora in Greece. Dozens of hot-air balloons that floated over the even more stunning rocks and caves of Cappadocia in Türkiye at sunrise. The surreally clear limestone lakes at Plitvice in Croatia, and the reunion with my motorcycle friends Claudia and Peter in Vienna, where they had moved back to a few months earlier.

My broken heart and the pain that had plagued me from the start of my adventures began to disappear into the background, and the bad memories with it. Finally, I could see that I hadn't only lost, I had also gained. Every lie he had told hadn't *just* been a lie, and every act of betrayal not *just* a betrayal. I had been right every single time, because I had sensed all the untruths from the start. I hadn't been crazy or paranoid. I could trust my gut feeling. It was the only thing that hadn't let me down. I welcomed my intuition with open arms, like an old friend. I had her back. And all the experiences and encounters of the past months had made her even stronger.

In Europe, I was no longer the exotic traveler, and I blended into the mixture of the masses of tourists and locals. Basanti, with her Indian plates, could still count on some interest, but she didn't seem to care one way or another. Part of me thought it was kind of amusing that as I got closer and closer to the Netherlands, I was being questioned differently. Where the questions used to be about my marital status, now they were about whether my motorcycle was suitable for me, why I mispronounced Hima-lyan, and if my trip had been even adventurous enough. After all, I hadn't camped along the way, and some people felt that was absolutely essential for something to be called an adventure.

One question remained the same throughout my entire journey: whether or not I was afraid, being a woman. Even after nine months on my motorcycle, I still didn't know how to respond to that. What did they mean, being a woman? These kinds of questions were impossible to answer without a control group. I had no way of finding out if my trip would have gone differently if I'd been a man. Just as I wasn't preoccupied with being hypothetically male, I wasn't consciously focused on being a woman either, or questioning how I experienced things as a woman. Who does that? I definitely didn't. Or did they mean I should have been afraid of men with bad intentions? That felt like a kick to the gut for all the men who had come to my aid everywhere, without even being asked. Who had carried my bags, righted my bike, carefully peeled my boots off my half-frozen feet, given me warm socks, replaced Basanti's clutch on their day off, or pushed me when she wouldn't start. No, I wasn't afraid of those men. True, I'd felt intimidated by the jeering, wolf-whistling men in Esfahan in Iran, but that one unpleasant moment paled in comparison to the overwhelming positive experiences. I had never truly been in danger there.

I spent less and less time in each country, until I rode through the final three countries from Austria in a single day. In order to leave again, I first had to go back. And so I did. I went back and pushed through to the Netherlands in one go. I tilted my head down one last time and gave Basanti's tank a loving pat with my left hand.

This faithful single cylinder, which I'd bought new for less than $2,400 in Delhi, had just safely carried me 22,370 miles across the world, and together we had seen twenty-five countries. I was proud of my friend.

Nobody would have thought we'd come this far, including me.

EPILOGUE

The journey from India to the Netherlands took only nine months, but it felt like I'd lived on the road for years. Every minute had counted for two, every impression had been larger than I'd been able to process. My family was waiting for me on the border between Belgium and the Netherlands. I hugged my mother, my father, and my little niece. It felt surreal to suddenly be able to speak my mother tongue again, out in the open on the street. I didn't have the heart to tell my parents what was really on my mind: that this had only been the beginning. Something had awoken inside me in Iran. Then I had reflected on it for months while riding. It was about who I'd been before I started this journey, who I was now, and how everything had changed.

I was the kid who'd been bullied at elementary school and desperately wanted to fit in at high school. I'd done jazz ballet, horse riding, and played the clarinet. I became a biologist and then a geologist. Full-time backpacker and then dredging superintendent. I was the daughter who was always away, the sister who became an aunt from afar, the friend who missed every birthday, and the weirdo who just went for it without nearly enough motorcycle experience.

But now I had become a woman who was both filmmaker and motorcycle adventurer. I had found what I'd been made to do all along. My years of roaming around as a solo-backpacking tourist had bored and exhausted me. Now I could travel alone, feeling utterly free, but still sharing it all through my videos. I could share the world as I saw it. Filmmaking felt like an insatiable hunger. No matter how much I devoured, I kept craving more. And unlike blogging, I had started making some money with my videos. I calculated that if I kept working hard, I'd be able to make a living with it in six months' time with a little luck.

From the moment I left Russia behind and turned toward Europe, a dotted line had started to take shape inside my head. A dotted line that should tame my hunger for adventure for a while: I would go from the southernmost point of the American continent, in Patagonia, to the northernmost point of Alaska on a motorcycle. From Patagonia to Alaska.

That didn't sound like such a terrible idea at all. I was ready.

ACKNOWLEDGMENTS

With this book, the dream I've carried since childhood has come true: I have become a writer.

I wrote a big portion of this book with a broken hand, after my bike and I took a tumble into a ditch at the Dinaric Rally in Croatia. I was not able nor allowed to ride my motorcycle for six weeks, and initially I didn't know what to do with myself for such a long period of time. But even though I couldn't ride, I found out I could still type with a broken hand. Imagine a Tyrannosaurus rex, that's pretty much what I looked like.

Most of all I want to thank my best friend, Mandy Alting, who drove me almost a thousand miles from Croatia back to the Netherlands, and supported and took care of me in those first few weeks when I couldn't do much besides write. Apart from being my absolute biggest traveling inspiration, she's always been there for me for the last fourteen years and without her, Itchy Boots would never have existed like it does today.

I also want to thank Maarten Basjes, my editor at Luitingh Sijthoff. You already believed in this book without ever having read a word I'd written in Dutch. This book wouldn't be here now if you hadn't sent me an email with the subject: "Talk about a book?" Your feedback and encouraging questions made me reflect more deeply about what it was I really wanted to say. We made the absolute most of it!

Thanks to proofreader Irmaria Pennekamp for her sharp criticism. Even though the feedback initially put me on my back foot, I had to admit you were right about many points and I wholeheartedly believe that the writing has improved because of it.

Heleen Westerman, thank you for your valuable help in straightening out my crooked sentences. You helped me with my English blogs for years as a writing coach, and it is always a pleasure to work with you! Your enthusiastic voice messages about how much you enjoyed another chapter of this book always gave me fresh motivation to keep writing.

Anique and Sander, thank you for reading the first draft, which was still so messy that I admire your bravery for daring to wrestle your way through it! Especially Anique's sharp eye kept surprising me, and I think you would fit right in at a publishing house!

Lots and lots of thanks to my lovely family and friends—thank you for your infinite understanding of the fact that I'm always away, and that even when I was there, I was often too busy writing to see you.

And then, of course, thank you to all the people who appeared in my life for a short period of time on this journey, and who helped me, in whatever way. The wonderful people I name in this book, who helped me pick Basanti up off the ground, who gave me shelter, food, and drink, and who gave me what I often needed the most: trust. Although this was a solo trip, and was meant to be one, it was the best people in India, Myanmar, Thailand, Malaysia, Oman, Dubai, Iran—and all the countries that followed—who made me laugh, supported me, and ensured that this trip could actually succeed.

I will never forget any of you.